D0504833

Dorset and the Sea

DORSET
AND
THE SEA

Gordon Le Pard

Dorset Books

First published in Great Britain in 2010

British Library Cataloguing-in-Publication Data
A CIP record for this title is available from the British Library

ISBN 978 1 871164 76 3

DORSET BOOKS
Dorset Books is a Partnership Between
Dorset County Council & Halsgrove

Halsgrove House,
Ryelands Industrial Estate,
Bagley Road, Wellington, Somerset TA21 9PZ
Tel: 01823 653777   Fax: 01823 216796
email: sales@halsgrove.com

Part of the Halsgrove group of companies
Information on all Halsgrove titles is available at: www.halsgrove.com

Printed and bound in Great Britain by SRP Ltd., Exeter

Contents

Introduction

I F YOU STAND on the end of the Cobb, the ancient harbour of Lyme Regis, and let your mind wander over the long history of the town, what do you see in your minds eye? The flat marshland, now long since lost to coastal erosion, dotted with huts and wreathed with smoke from the salt works that stood there thirteen hundred years ago, or perhaps smoke from a different source, as the town burns when the Royalists attack during the Civil War. Can you imagine ships arriving from Africa, and the crew of the *Princess* striding along the Cobb with elephants tusks on their shoulders, or perhaps some of the people associated with Lyme Regis, the slim shape of Jane Austen, walking the Cobb and imagining where Louisa Musgrove was to fall, or the young Mary Anning, basket in hand setting out to find the fossils which would make her, and Lyme Regis, famous. Or the two military men, Captain D'Arcy and Colonel Fanshawe who took their skill at building defences against the enemy, and turned it to building defences against the sea, creating the Cobb we see today.

It is this multi-layered aspect of the history of the Dorset coast and sea that is celebrated here. The book is arranged around themes, rather than places, so in one place you will find how the town of Weymouth was devastated by the French, and in about how she grew into the great tourist destination today.

Some aspects of the coast are not covered in detail – the Second World War only gets a passing mention, as other writers have looked at it in greater detail, though the stories told here might be unfamiliar to some. Others are dealt with more fully as they are stories that deserve to be better known, the amazing tale of the Pirates of Purbeck or the courage of Ann Davison of Portland for example.

Above all take this opportunity to explore the coast, you never know what you might find. *[Some years ago I was walking on the coast near the old cliff quarries at Winspit when I met an alien. It was several months before I discovered where it had come from. That autumn Dr Who revealed that, instead of being nineteenth century quarries, the caves at Winspit actually lead to the underground city of the Daleks!]*

Gordon Le Pard
Weymouth
2010

1: The Dorset Coast

DORSET IS A MARITIME COUNTY with a remarkable and unusual coastline. The first, and perhaps most curious fact is that there is serious disagreement as to how long the Dorset coast is. Two figures are given, 142 and 285 km. The difference is simply this, when measuring the coast do you draw the line across the entrance to Poole Harbour, or do you follow the coastline around the harbour, for the shore of the harbour is, though it seems difficult to believe, one kilometre longer than the length of the coast, from Highcliffe to Lyme Regis, going straight across the mouth of Poole Harbour.

Then there is the coastline itself. The Dorset coast is amazingly diverse, with examples of just about every type of coastal landform found in Britain. High cliffs of hard rock, low cliffs of soft rock, sandy beaches and sand dunes, pebble beaches and salt marsh, estuaries and lagoons, Dorset seems to have it all.

Beginning in the east there are soft, low cliffs of sand and clay that run from Chewton Bunny to Highcliffe. A 'Bunny' is nothing to do with a rabbit, it is a dialect word for a short valley that runs down towards the coast; as you head westward the name changes and these features are called 'Chines'. These soft cliffs are rich in fossils and for the first time in Dorset, but by no means the last, the coast is very important for geology. The cliffs are of

Chewton Bunny, a narrow gap in the cliffs which marks the eastern edge of the county of Dorset.

Looking as though they had just been washed up by the sea, these fossils are about 40 million years old.

Right: Only a narrow strip of grass separates Highcliffe Castle from the eroding cliff edge.

Eocene age (about 40 million years old) and were laid down in a warm sub tropical sea. Sharks teeth are common as are numerous shells, these can be so well preserved that they erode from the cliffs and lie on the beach mixed up with modern ones, only their grey colour and unusual shapes distinguish them from shells of creatures living today.

The cliff drops rapidly to a spit of land called, appropriately enough, Mudeford (pronounced muddy-ford) and the entrance to Christchurch Harbour. This is narrow and difficult to negotiate, some charts advise that it should not be entered without local knowledge! Inside the harbour is dominated by the bulk of Warren Hill on Hengistbury Head, which forms its south western side. Scarred by quarrying, it protects the harbour and, by sheltering part of the harbour from the prevailing south westerly winds, can make things interesting for the small boat sailor. On the north eastern side the low hills are now covered with houses, merging into the grassland of Stanpit Marsh which forms the north western side of the harbour. On the northern side a channel runs up towards Purewell, this was once much wider and small vessels could sail up to a landing place now lost in the reeds. Mother

Christchurch lies inland, some way from the sea. This etching show Christchurch Harbour and Hengistbury Head from the tower of the priory church.

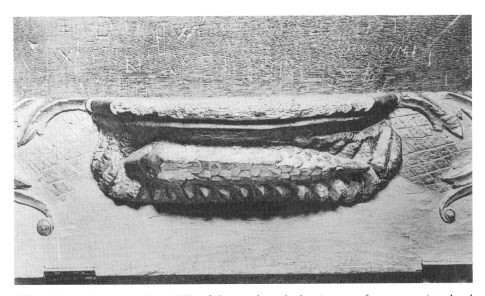

The River Avon at Christchurch has long been famous for its salmon. In the early fifteenth century one was carved on a misericord in the Priory Church.

Siller's Channel runs into the middle of the marsh, and takes its name from a notorious local pub landlady who was in league with the local smugglers. The southernmost channel is the one to take, snaking through the reeds it eventually brings the sailor to Christchurch Quay.

Christchurch lies on the junction of two rivers, the Avon and the Stour. The Stour runs north east into Dorset, through Wimborne Minster, Blandford Forum and Gillingham, and so to its source at Stourhead, just across the county boundary in Wiltshire. The Avon too rises in Wiltshire, at Bishops Cannings, only a few miles from the source of the Bristol Avon. This is a much greater river and was once navigable all the way to Salisbury, as well as people travelling up the river it has long been famous for its salmon, which still make the journey upriver to spawn. A salmon is carved on one of the medieval misericords (wooden seats) in the Priory Church.

These two rivers now flow into the sea at Christchurch Harbour, but not so long ago, during the last Ice Age, they were tributaries of a river that flowed westwards down the Solent, rising in Poole Harbour at the junction of the Frome and the Piddle and running into the sea somewhere south of Selsey Bill. The Isle of Wight lay at the end of a peninsula, an extension of the present Isle of Purbeck and the River Solent flowed down a broad valley that ran from Poole Bay, across Christchurch Bay where the Avon and Frome joined it then along the Solent to a junction with the Meon and Itchen off the entrance to

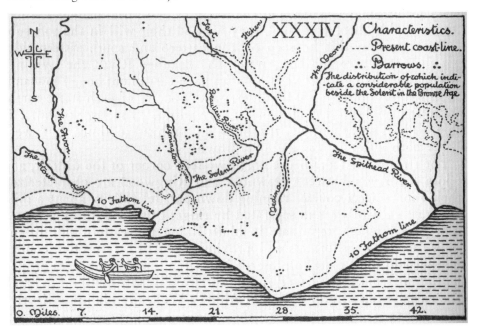

A slightly fanciful map of the River Solent, drawn in 1915. This shows the situation just before the Isle of Wight became an island.

A small Palaeolithic hand axe, perhaps as much as 500,000 years old, from the Bournemouth gravels.

The beach at Studland in the 1950s. Once a wild area where Marconi carried out some of his earliest radio experiments. This is now, notoriously, the location of some of the most expensive houses in Britain.

Southampton Water. After the Ice Age ended, about 11000BC, the rising sea broke through the chalk ridge that linked the Isle of Wight to the Isle of Purbeck. The valley flooded quickly. For a time the Frome and Piddle may have flowed out to sea through this gap in the chalk ridge, whilst the Avon and Frome flowed down a truncated River Solent. But this situation didn't last long and the sea quickly eroded a channel down the Solent, permanently separating the Isle of Wight from the mainland.

Turning west from Hengistbury Head the coastline rises again to a series of soft clay cliffs, now covered with houses from Southbourne to Boscombe to Bournemouth, Branksome, Canford Cliffs and so to Sandbanks and the entrance to Poole Harbour. These cliffs are also of Eocene date, similar to those east of Christchurch, and used to be famous for their rich fossil flora. Sadly the development of sea defences and the long coastal promenade have obscured these deposits and fossil leaves are now rarely found. They are interesting in showing that the area had a strange mixture of warm temperate and tropical flora, warm enough in the summer to let tropical plants grow, but never cold enough in the winter to kill them, climatic conditions that do not occur today anywhere on earth. These cliffs are capped with much younger gravel that contains some of the earliest traces of man in the county in the form of stone tools. These gravels may have been laid down by earlier versions of the River Solent that flowed during earlier Ice Ages and Interglacials (the warm periods between Ice Ages). Off Bournemouth a relic of the old valley of the River Solent can be found in the form of a 'fossil forest':

'I must, however mention the existence of a submerged forest, occasionally visible at low water, at the foot of the cliffs at Bournemouth, which seems to show that there, as elsewhere, a depression of a former land surface has taken place. Mr Albert Way, F.S.A., who has had the opportunity of examining some of the stumps of the trees exposed at rare intervals at low water, informs me that they appear to be those of the true Scotch fir; and also that local tradition speaks of an impassable morass having, so late as the commencement of the present century, intervened between the line of the cliffs and the sea. On occasion of one of my visits to Bournemouth, some of these stumps were

The chain ferry
between Sandbanks
and Studland, across
the entrance to
Poole Harbour. This
vessel, photographed
in 1931, is just one
of the many ferries
which have operated
on this important
route.

fortunately visible, and were pointed out to me by Mr. Way at a spot but a few
yards west of the pier, and between high and low-water mark.'

Sandbanks is now famous, or infamous, for its property prices: some of the most expensive
houses in the county are to be found here.

At the end of the Sandbanks spit is the chain ferry that carries cars across the entrance
to Poole Harbour to the Studland Peninsula. However following the longer version of the
Dorset coast into the harbour, and around the coast the shoreline is heavily developed with
houses and numerous marinas and smaller landing places for pleasure craft. This coast is
well protected and has grown over the years, indeed at Baiter, on the edge of Poole, the
whole shoreline is artificial, having been reclaimed from the sea in the past 150 years. The
old town of Poole lies at the entrance to Holes Bay, one of two harbours within the harbour.
A narrow entrance under Poole bridge, the bay soon opens out into a wide sheltered area
of water, much of which is covered in mud flats. Progressing north the bay becomes less
and less accessible owing to the shallow water until north of the railway line, which crosses
the bay on a causeway, there is very little access for boats at all.

West of Poole the Hamworthy coast is the most industrial in Dorset with the
continental Ferry Terminal, however this soon ends and the coast swings north again under
the railway bridge and into Lytchett Bay. Apart from a few houses on the south eastern side
this bay, the second, and smaller, of the 'harbours within the harbour', is one of the quietest
and least accessible parts of Poole Harbour. Extensive mud flats surround the small islands
on the western side of the bay which, together with long low embankments, remains of long
failed land reclamation schemes, make access difficult.

From the entrance to Lytchett Bay there is a long low coast, bordered with trees which
cover the banks of sea defences almost all the way down the Wareham channel to the mouth
of the Frome, the way to the ancient port of Wareham.

The complex and
beautiful coastline
of the south western
corner of Poole
Harbour.

The Frome has been contained between two high banks, and snakes from side to side making an interesting and attractive approach to the town, though virtually impossible now for any commercial craft, apart from small sightseeing boats.

Leaving the mouth of the Frome, back into Poole Harbour, now following the southern shore of the Wareham channel, here there are first long low banks of sea defences, followed by low gravel cliffs, for mile after mile there is little or no trace of modern man, few houses or any other buildings. Deep inlets between heathland, woodland and occasional meadows, make this area a rich habitat for wildlife. Also in this quiet, south west corner of the harbour, are the small islands, Long Island, Round Island, Green Island, and Furzey, all privately owned and quiet, apart from Furzey, which is the base for the oil drilling and pumping from the Dorset oilfields, but it is so well landscaped and hidden within the woodland of the island, that, apart from the large, modern and well maintained pier there is nothing to distinguish Furzey Island from the others.

Green and Furzey Islands both show signs of erosion on their western sides. This is also obvious on Brownsea the largest of the islands, and the one with the most complex history. It has been a haunt of Vikings, priests and pirates the base for one of the earliest chemical industries in the country, heavily industrialised to make pottery drainpipes, farmed for daffodils and abandoned to nature. Now it is a wildlife reserve and popular tourist destination.

These islands of Poole Harbour have long fascinated people. In 1612 Michael Drayton wrote a wonderful, bizarre account of the three islands (Furzey, Brownsea called Brunksey and Green called Saint Helen's) in his topographical poem *Polyolbion*.

Brownsea and her daughter islands, Furzey, Green, Long and Round, nestled in the south western corner of Poole Harbour.

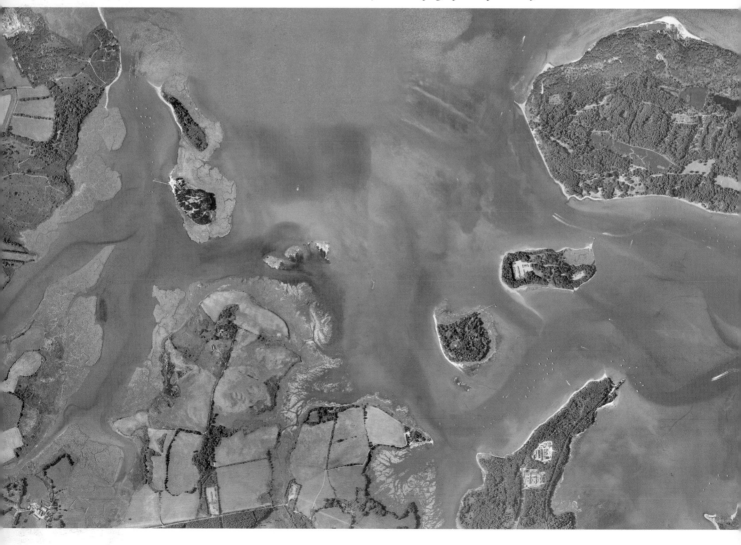

When *Poole* was young, a lusty sea-born lass,
Great *Albion* to this Nymph an earnest suitor was ;
And bare himself so well, and so in favour came,
That he in little time, upon this lovely dame,
Begot three maiden Isles, his darlings and delight :
The eldest, *Brunksey* call'd ; the second, *Fursey* hight ;
The youngest and the last, and lesser than the other,
Saint *Helen's* name doth bear, the darling of her mother.
And, for the goodly *Poole* was one of *Thetis'* train,
Who scorn'd a Nymph of hers her virgin-band should stain.
Great *Albion* (that forethought, the angry Goddess would
Both on the dam and brats take what revenge she could)
I' th' bosom of the *Poole* his little children plac'd :
First *Brunksey* ; *Fursey* next ; and little *Helen* last ;
Then, with his mighty arms doth clip the *Poole* about,
To keep the angry Queen, fierce *Amphitrite*, out.
Against whose lordly might she musters up her waves ;
And strongly thence repuls'd (with madness) scolds and raves.

Leaving Poole there is one curious myth to consider; it is often stated that Poole Harbour is the second largest harbour in the world after Sydney Harbour. This has been current for many years, certainly since the 1940s. How it came about is unknown, as it is simply untrue. Geographers might disagree exactly what constitutes a harbour, but however one is defined there are many larger than Poole. It can claim to be the largest in Britain and that should be enough, even for such an exceptional coastline as that of Dorset.

Leaving Poole Harbour the coast swings west and then south, a low coastline of sand dunes. This is the youngest part of the Dorset coast. Within the Studland peninsula lies a small freshwater lake called Little Sea; it is freshwater today but one hundred and fifty years ago it was still linked to the 'Big Sea'; two hundred and fifty years ago it was a bay. The growth of the Studland Peninsula is a textbook example of coastal gain.

The ground slowly rises around the ancient village of Studland, then, quite suddenly the white chalk cliffs begin to climb. These chalk cliffs mark the beginning of the 'Jurassic

Little Sea, in the seventeenth century a bay, in the nineteenth century a tidal inlet and now a freshwater pond.

The chalk cliffs of Ballard Down (Bollard in 1882) run east west and end in the chalk stacks of Old Harry.

Coast' World Heritage Site, from here to the Devon border the rocks get progressively older. Here the chalk rapidly rises to 116 metres, whilst off shore there is a wonderful group of sea stacks and sea arches, culminating in the sea stack 'Old Harry'. Up until 1896 Old Harry had a companion, his 'Wife': this fell as part of the natural process that has been going on since the sea broke through the chalk ridge that linked the Isle of Purbeck to the Isle of Wight.

The chalk cliffs of Ballard Down continue until they drop down in the approach to Swanage Bay, here there was once an estuary that ran under where Swanage railway station now stands, which was finally filled in during the early nineteenth century as the town began it rapid growth, first as a port for the export of stone, later as a holiday resort. Leaving Swanage, past Peveril Point one element of the development of Swanage as a resort stands out clearly on the cliff top, Durlston Castle. This sham castle was built in 1887 by George Burt as a centrepiece for his development of the hills to the south of Swanage. Much of the development never took place but his park on the hill top with educational plaques, Durlston Castle and the Great Globe, a ten foot wide model of the Earth, survives as Durlston County Park, a development of which George Burt would probably fully approve.

High on the cliffs, west of the Anvil Point lighthouse, stands a metal pylon, marking the beginning of a measured nautical mile. Ships can run parallel to the coast and, by observing exactly when the vessel passed each pylon, the exact speed could be calculated and so the ships log could be accurately calibrated.

The mill pond in Swanage once lay at the end of a tidal creek where ships could moor at the back of the old houses.

The high stone cliffs run for miles after mile, broken where valleys run down to the sea, and with occasional bays. The cliffs have been quarried for centuries and the galleries and platforms of the former quarries are prominent features, until St Aldhelm's head is reached, crowned by its ancient chapel. From here the colour of the rocks begins to change, until at Kimmeridge they are dark grey, this is the famous Kimmeridge shale which has also been exploited for centuries.

Hard rocks return and high cliffs until Worbarrow Bay, overtopped by the magnificent Flowers Barrow and its crumbling hill fort. Beyond the cliffs run lower now, backed by the ridge of Bindon Hill to the most famous bay in Dorset, Lulworth Cove.

This curious, almost circular, bay cut by the sea punching through a band of much

Lulworth Cove, here photographed in the 1920s, was described at the time as the most perfect bay in England.

Durdle Door, a remarkable sea arch, is said to be the most photographed feature on the south coast of England, here drawn in an eighteenth century engraving.

harder rock and eroding the softer chalk behind, has long been one of the most famous features of the coast – tourists have been coming here for centuries. Just along from the cove a tiny sea arch leads into a small bay. This is Stair Hole, which gives some idea of how Lulworth Cove began, the harder rock being pierced and a bay eroding behind. This would make the Stair Hole interesting enough, but it is surpassed by the amazing rock to on the eastern side of the Hole, twisted and distorted, which is known to Geologists as the 'Lulworth Crumple'. This rock, whose 'steps' give Stair Hole its name, provides eloquent testimony to the immense forces which have bent, twisted and distorted the rocks of the Dorset coast over many millennia.

Leaving Stair Hole it is little more than a mile to Man O'War Bay, so called from the supposed similarity of the long rock in the middle of the bay to a warship, and the most famous feature of the Dorset coast, Durdle Door. This massive sea arch must be the most photographed point on the entire coast, it is certainly the standard image of the Dorset coast, reproduced in countless forms throughout the world.

Now the cliffs rise again to the magnificent heights of Bats Head, pieced at the bottom by a tiny arch, the 'Eye of the Monster'. These wonderful cliffs continue to White Nothe

The high cliffs running west from Lulworth Cove towards Weymouth.

(Nose). Then dropping in a tumble of broken undercliffs to Osmington. Two hundred years ago these were famous as the 'burning cliffs':

> In the autumn of 1826 vapour began to rise from the rifts and crannies of what a contemporary writer with a fine flow of language and a penchant for capital letters, calls "a scene wasteful and wild as Chaos, where stillness reigns, and Great Nature dwells in awful solitude." It was not at first very much of a conflagration, for the smoke is described as having been " as much as is usually caused at the lighting of a common fire," but it would, nevertheless, appear to have been rather awesome to that writer, for he goes on to describe how the smoke "on a calm day has been seen to rise slowly and with peculiar grandeur, forming a majestic column at least 20 feet in height, producing a curious and imposing effect." He evidently possessed the journalistic instinct for effective exaggeration.
>
> This wonder brought many marvel-hunters to see it, and, probing and scratching about, to discover the source of the fire, they brought down an overhanging piece of cliff that for a time smothered, but did not extinguish it; for, when Baggs [the cottager who lived on the cliffs] went to dig in his garden, on May 15th, 1827, he dug into a cavern of fire like a red-hot kiln. Then the cliff burst into a flame and so continued for some months, like a miniature Vesuvius, converting Weymouth Bay by day and night into a closer resemblance to the Bay of Naples than ever before contemplated by travellers.

The geological curiosities continue at Osmington where a steep slipway runs to the sea, here is the only waterfall on the coast where a small stream runs over a low cliff into the sea. The cliffs continue, soft and tumbled round Osmington Bay, rising as Preston is approached then dropping to sea level at Lodmoor. Now, for the first time since Swanage, human development dominates the coast, from the sea wall at Lodmoor to the first houses of Weymouth, and then the sweep of Weymouth Bay. Houses line the sea front, in front runs the esplanade, and in front of that is an extensive sand beach, protected from the south by the Nothe Peninsula, now crowned by a massive Victorian fort. Here, is the entrance to Weymouth Harbour, the smallest of the major harbours on the Dorset coast. Curiously this harbour has narrowed and got smaller over the centuries as the provision for shipping has improved!

From Weymouth the shoreline runs into Portland Harbour, or follows the breakwater

The *Cyclorarma* is a remarkable view of the coast, drawn in a single strip from Lulworth Cove to Portland Bill.

directly to Portland. Here the cliffs rise above a tumbled undercliff, known as the West Wears, a similar area on the other side of the Island is, sensibly enough, known as the East Wears. The cliff is crowned by the Verne Citadel, a massive Victorian fortification now a prison. High cliffs with tumbled rocks and vegetation continue for several miles, with occasional small landing places marked by boat cranes, a distinctive feature of Portland, adapted from the cranes originally used to load stone into boats. Many of these rocks are roughly shaped, abandoned blocks from the cliff-top quarries, for Portland stone is simply one of the finest building stones on earth. Portland slopes southward, at the northern end the cliffs are 100 metres above the sea, by the time Portland Bill is reached the rocks are only two or three metres above the water. This wedge shape is very distinctive from the sea and has been a landmark for centuries. The Bill, as it is called has been clearly marked to sailors by the lighthouse and earlier sea mark. Off the Bill the water is never calm, this is the notorious Portland race, a area of troubled water from which sailors have been well advised to keep clear for centuries.

The western shore of Portland is, if possible, even more unfriendly than the eastern. The cliffs run almost vertically into the sea; there are small bays and coves, but these are more geographical features than places where boats can land. The cliffs rise again, until at the northern end of the island there are more tumbled undercliffs, the West Wears before a proper beach appears at Chesil Cove.

View of Portland, taken about five miles SW¾W from the Bill. It has nearly the same Bill-like appearance when seen from the Eastward.

Lights

Portland from the sea as shown on a chart of 1787, the wedge shape is particularly clear.

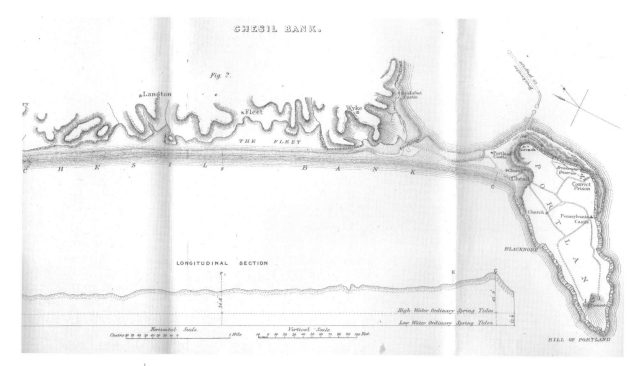

Chesil Beach runs parallel to the coast from Portland to Abbotsbury, behind Chesil Beach lies the Fleet Lagoon.

Chesil Cove is the only place for many miles where boats can attempt to make a landing, which is why there are over sixty recorded shipwrecks here. From here the coast has a different, unique, aspect. For the next eight, twelve or fifteen miles the coastline is dominated by Chesil Beach.

Chesil Beach is unique in Britain, a long shingle beach that links the Isle of Portland to the mainland. The disagreement as to its length is due to a lack of agreement as to the western end of the beach. The eastern end, in Chesil Cove, is clear enough, but where is the western end? At Abbotsbury where Chesil beach meets the land or at West Bay where the small estuary of the River Bride makes a natural break in the coast, or somewhere in between.

There are many curious features about Chesil, the grading of the shingle being the strangest. At West Bay there is a sandy beach, the sand is coarser at Burton Bradstock, pea sized shingle at Abbotsbury, medium sixed pebbles at Ferrybridge and stones the size of a fist at Chesil Cove. The waves, which have carried out this natural sorting, have also given Chesil Beach its profile, dropping steeply into the sea. Waves breaking here can create an undertow which will make it very difficult, if not impossible, for a swimmer to safely get to the beach. Few local people will ever risk bathing off Chesil.

The unfriendly seaward side of Chesil Beach as shown in a nineteenth century engraving. The wrecked ships are not an exaggeration, this is one of the most dangerous stretches of coast in Britain.

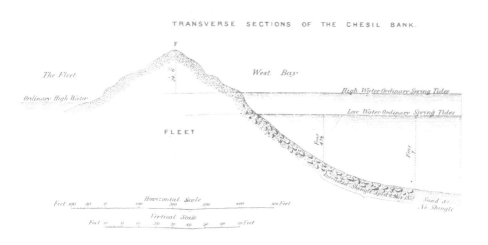

TRANSVERSE SECTIONS OF THE CHESIL BANK.

The Fleet

West Bay

High Water Ordinary Spring Tides

Ordinary High Water

Low Water Ordinary Spring Tides

FLEET

Horizontal Scale

Vertical Scale

The profile of Chesil Beach. The steep seaward face is one of the reasons the beach is so dangerous.

From the sea the beach dominates the view, the low hills behind have few recognisable landmarks, which is why St Catherine's Chapel at Abbotsbury is so important. It provides a recognisable feature that can enable a sailor to gain some knowledge as to where he is off the beach. Local fishermen used the size of the pebbles to get a rough idea as to where they were.

Behind the beach lies the Fleet, a long tidal lagoon, almost fresh water at the Abbotsbury end where there has been a Swannery since at least 1354, when the Abbot was reported for selling swans to his relatives at bargain prices. The Swannery still thrives though as a tourist attraction, the swans are no longer kept for the pot, though their feathers still provide calligraphers with the finest quills, just as they did in the time of the Abbey. Michael Drayton also noted the Swannery, his bizarre account, whilst accurately describing the Fleet as being filled with 'oozy pools', also mentions "naked Sea-Nymphs", which no one else has, perhaps sadly, ever seen again.

> Not sever'd from the shore, aloft where *Chesill* lifts
> Her ridged snake-like sands, in wrecks and smould'ring drifts,
> Which by the South-wind rais'd, are heav'd on little hills :
> Whose valleys with his flows when foaming *Neptune* fills,
> Upon a thousand swans the naked Sea-Nymphs ride
> Within the oozy pools, replenish'd every tide

There are many theories as to the origin of Chesil Beach, however one clue can be found in the blocks of peat that are thrown onto the beach during winter storms. Wood leaves of Reed Mace and the bones of a European Beaver have been found. Where the Chesil Beach now stands was once a fresh water marsh (beavers wont live in salt or brackish water). The peat dates from about 4500 BC, when people were already living along the margins of the marsh that was to become the Fleet.

Beyond West Bexington there is Burton Mere, a reed-fringed pool behind the beach. This is a strange place which may, or may not, be a relic of a larger and longer Fleet.

Chesil Beach at the Abbotsbury end in the late nineteenth century, when sheep grazed the shingle vegetation.

Bones of European Beaver. These were found in a block of peat which was washed onto the beach at Abbotsbury. They derive from a peat bed that lies off-shore. This was laid down 6,000 years ago when Chesil Beach lay well to the south with a freshwater marsh behind it.

Right: Hive Beach at Burton Bradstock. The cliffs were used as a training area during the second world war. Hive has nothing to do with bees, it comes for the Old English Hythe meaning a landing place.

Ammonites in a house wall at Lyme Regis, the iconic symbol of the town.

Cliffs start rising again cut by narrow valleys at Burton Hive and Burton Freshwater, before the wider gap at West Bay. For centuries this was known as Bridport Harbour or Bridport Haven until the railway arrived in 1884, when the Great Western Railway's publicity people decided that West Bay was more likely to attract tourists than Bridport Harbour and named the station accordingly. The power of the railway was such that in due course the harbour's name changed. This had a knock on effect out at sea as, for centuries the large bay that ran from Portland to Beer Head was known as 'West Bay', this could now be confused with the town, so the bay's name was changed as well, it is now known as 'Lyme Bay'.

Immediately off West Bay ancient trees were once to be found. The first reference was by John Hutchins in 1774 who wrote:

> Some years since, [there was] an extraordinary reflux of the sea at Bridport mouth, when nine or ten stumps and roots of large trees two, or three feet in diameter and three feet high, appeared, but were never seen since.

More recently divers saw these tree trunks, to the west of the harbour mouth, when the sediment has uncovered them. They may not exist any longer as they may have been buried when the new harbour wall was built. This isn't certain as they were looked for before the new wall was built but couldn't be found.

Beyond Bridport the cliffs rise again, with gaps at Seatown, below Chideock, and at Charmouth. The cliffs now are fossil rich, and are one of the most famous fossil hunting locations in the world. Ammonites and belemnites are common and remains of the great marine reptiles, ichthyosaurs and plesiosaurs are occasionally found. The cliffs rise to the height of 191 metres, at Golden Cap, one of the highest points on the south coast of England. Beyond Golden Cap is Black Ven, the largest active mud slide in Europe, a very dangerous place, though fascinating for geologists. Finally the cliffs tumble to the sea again to the tiny, fascinating, port of Lyme Regis.

Lyme Regis is probably the most famous town on the Dorset coast. Virtual birthplace of the science of palaeontology, where great discoveries are still being made and a key point in England's only natural World Heritage Site, the Jurassic Coast. It is the setting of one of the greatest novels in the English language, and the surprising inspiration of many other works of art and literature. The western edge of this gem of a town is also the western edge of the County of Dorset and aptly beings this brief description of the coast to an end.

2: A Living from the Sea

A FEW YEARS AGO a statue was erected just below Portland heights where the main road snakes its way up the precipitous slope onto the top of the Island. Entitled, 'The Spirit of Portland', it cleverly depicts a fisherman and a quarryman, harking back to the two ancient trades of the island. But these are not just the ancient trades of Portland, they are the ancient trades of the inhabitants of the coast of Dorset.

The spirit of Portland – The Mason.

The spirit of
Portland – The
Fisherman.

Above and below: Small
boat anchors found
off the Purbeck
Coast. Similar
anchors have been
found in the
Romano-British
settlement at Cleavel
Point.

FISHING

Probably as soon as there were people living on the Dorset coast there were people fishing.
In one of the earliest coastal communities discovered, the Mesolithic (Middle Stone Age)
site at Culverswell on Portland, dating from about 5400BC, the people seemed to have
eaten vast quantities of shellfish, particularly limpets. The conditions were not good for the
preservation of bone, but a few fish bones were found including Whiting, a common inshore
fish, and Ling a highly prized food fish, whose liver produces oil which has been used for
lighting and medicinal purposes. Both these two species of fish could have been caught in
in-shore waters using hand lines, or from some sea-going craft such as a dug-out canoe.

Later sites have not provided fish-bones, but this is more likely due to the fragile nature
of the bones, rather than that the people weren't fishing. In the middle Iron Age (350 BC)
cockle shells are common on the sites around Poole Harbour, later winkles and oysters
were added to the diet. The discovery of small boat anchors, and what appear to be net
weights, in the settlement at Cleavel Point in Poole Harbour, would suggest that people were
also fishing in the Iron Age. Similarly there is little direct Roman evidence of fishing, apart
from the large number of oyster shells found on most Roman sites, indeed oysters are
almost indicative of a Roman site. There is a story that the massive Roman villa at
Rockbourne, in Hampshire but on a tributary of the Avon, was discovered when a poacher
found a mass of oysters when digging out a rabbit (an amateur archaeologist overheard him
talking about it in a pub and got the location of the villa for a couple of pints!). Since
Poole was famous in later years for it oysters, and was the location of a substantial Roman

settlement, it is reasonable to assume that many of the oysters found on Dorset sites originally came from the harbour.

As soon as there are written records, the importance of fishing becomes apparent. In 1086, the Domesday Book records that at Lyme Regis:

Fishermen rent it and pay 15 shillings to the monks for the privilege of fishing.

Whilst two hundred and fifty years later the fisheries of Portland paid the considerable sum of £10 to the king. At Abbotsbury the local fishermen paid the Abbey in kind, some of the fishes caught were always given to the Abbot. The last Abbot of Abbotsbury, who became vicar of Abbotsbury after the dissolution of the Abbey, noted that;

> Also the custombe hath byn that the Vicar of Abbotsbury shulde have for his own sustenaunce ev'ry Sat'day wykely all such fish that the fishermen did take, that is to say, if they did cant [sell by auction] or alloot [share out] ther fish at the sea side then the Vicar should have a cant or alloot as one of thez had [the vicar should have an equal share with the fishermen]. And if case be that they fishermen did sell ther fishe. Being it of ony sortt of fishe, then the Xth [tenth] of the same to remayne to the lorde or parsons use ... and therefo' ye fynd them ther dinner, and on Saynt Thom's Eve befor Cristmas a barell of ayle and one dosyn cakes wt other spices

Whilst in later years a story also referred to this custom and the, by then traditional, greed of the monks:

> It appears that the Bay of Weymouth [once] produced the Pilcher [pilchard], which is now rarely caught beyond the coast of Cornwall, for the Holy Fraternity of Benedictine Monks at Abbotsbury, the fishermen on the estate were obliged to furnish the monastery with the first caught fish, every morning. [Then] a shrewd and penetrating owner of a boat, discovered, that a word had been inserted in their written tenures, on which a notable quibble might be raised, and accordingly, one morning, the body of fishermen presented themselves before the door of the Monastery, and gave the porter, three small pilchers; the monks instantly rose, and demanded the motive of this unparalleled insult on their lords; the fishermen observed that the quantity was without any doubt small, but that by the strict letter of their feudal tenures they were only bound to deliver the first caught, and they had performed this by tendering to the brotherhood the three pilchers.

In 1987 archaeologists in Poole found the remains of a boatyard dating to about 1400. Numerous ships timbers were preserved in the wet mud, and from them it was possible to reconstruct a small medieval fishing boat. To everyone's surprise the reconstruction was very similar to a larger version of the traditional Lerret, this is a large rowing boat (though in the past some were adapted to take a sail) about fifteen feet long. It is clinker built (the upper plank overlapping the lower) and double ended, with apparently two bows. The rowers seats are positioned so that the men can change position and row forward or backward equally easily, it is notoriously strong, it has to be as it has to cope with landing on Chesil Beach.

As well as the evidence from the design, there is documentary evidence that the Lerret is a very old type of boat. The earliest mention of a lerret comes in the records of Weymouth town council, in 1615:

> [Hire of] 2 Lerretts to save the towne boatt from castinge awaye £0 7s 4d

Fishing for Mackerel along Chesil Beach. This scene didn't change for centuries. It was described by Daniel Defoe at the beginning of the eighteenth century and photographed at the beginning of the twentieth.

And on June 24, 1618

> Examination of W. Knott, Christmas Peters and others about taking three
> men in a *Lirret* on board a barque in the Roads [Weymouth Bay], said to be
> bound for Bristowe [Bristol] … It appeared unto Mr Mayor that the barque
> was a pirate vessel.

However in many places you will find it recorded that the word Lerret derives from the
first of her kind, which was called the *Lady of Loretto* which was built in 1682, but the earliest
mention of a Lerret is in 1615, so where does this story come from?

In 1849 the Royal Navy carried out a survey of the local forms of boat from around
the British coast in order to identify good designs. In the report on the Lerret this letter,
from Captain Manning of Portland Castle, is included.

> Many years ago I was particularly anxious to discover, if possible, the meaning
> and origin of the term "lerret", as applied to the boats here, and after much
> research, which occupied some considerable period, I obtained the following
> information from a very respectable old man named Pearce, who died about
> 18 years since, and who for many years had commanded merchant vessels
> trading between the port of London and the Mediterranean. One day, while
> in conversation with Pearce, he was giving me an account of his having been
> caught in a heavy squall in the Gulf of Venice, and, being compelled to put
> into Anconca, his vessel much disabled. During the progress of spinning his
> long yarn and talking of Anconca, he said "I conclude you are aware why our
> Portland boats are called lerrets", and on my expressing my ignorance, but at
> the same time wishing to obtain information on the subject, he proceeded as
> follows.

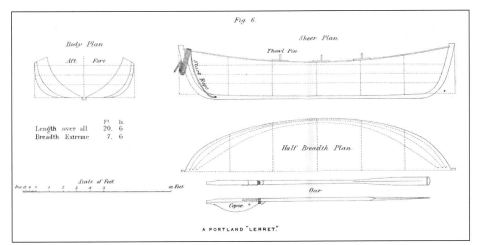

Drawings of the Lerret made by Sir John Coode in the 1850s.

> "Upwards of 100 years since, as I have been informed, a Portland man
> was master of a vessel trading to Anconca, and while there was induced to
> pay a visit to the far-famed 'Lady of Loreto, or Loretto': the gorgeous finery
> of which made such an impression on his mind, that after his retirement
> from the toils and troubles of a maritime life, he came to reside in his native
> village – Chesil – and had a particularly fine boat built, which was a great
> improvement on the boats then in use here and to which he gave the name
> 'Lady of Loretto'" and, Pearce went on to say that at some future date he
> would show me a paper to convince me that there was some foundation for
> the tale he had related. Accordingly, about three weeks afterwards Pearce,

who was at the time about 80 years of age and a great martyr to rheumatism, sent a message to me to the effect that if I would call upon him he had something to show me. On my proceeding to his residence, he produced a curious old document, called a "Church gift" (a certain description of conveyance of real and personal property where the Law of Gravelkind is in operation, as is the case in this island) dated as far back, if my memory does not fail me, as 1682, and amongst other property mentioned in the said deed of conveyance was the following:

'I also give to my son John my boat, with all her gear, called "The Lady of Loretto". I have not the slightest doubt but that the term "lerret" as applied to the boats here, is a corruption of the word Loretto, taken in connection with the circumstances I have related.

signed Charles Augustus Manning

The Lerret, a medieval boat that survived to the present.

So what are we to make of the story. First we cannot be sure how much is accurate, it was written at least eighteen years after the conversation took place, so details such as dates cannot be trusted. We also know that there was a type of boat called a Lerret already in existence many years before the events in the story are supposed to have happened. If the events in the story are more or less correct, then what probably happened was this.

The retired captain built a boat in the 1680s, which he called the *Lady of Loretto*, thinking the name an excellent one for a Lerret. As for the boat being a new design, people were constantly arguing over and improving the design of the Lerret, right up until it began to fall out of use in the 1930s, so they were probably doing the same three hundred years ago.

The Lerrets were used to catch fish off Chesil it a very particular fashion, first described by Daniel Defoe in 1724. In the summer of that year he was travelling along the coast road from Abbotsbury to Bridport:

Here we saw boats all the way on the shore fishing for mackerell, which they take in the easiest manner imaginable; for they fix one end of the net to a pole, set deep into the sand, then the net being in a boat, they row right out into the water some length, then turn, and row parallel with the shore, veering out the net all the while, till they have let go all the net, except the line at the end, and then the boat rows on shore, when the men haling the net to the shore at both ends, bring to shore with it such fish, as they surrounded in the little way they rowed; this, at that time, proved to be an incredible number, insomuch, that the men could hardly draw them on shore: As soon as the boats had brought their fish on shore, we observed a guard, or watch, placed on the shore in several places, who we found had their eye not on the fishermen, but on the country people, who came down to the shore to buy their fish; and very sharp we found they were; and some that came with small carts were obliged to go back empty, without any fish. When we came to enquire into the particulars of this, we found, that these were officers placed on the shore by the justices and magistrates of the towns about, who were order'd to prevent the country farmers buying the mackerell to dung their land with them, which was thought to be dangerous, as to infection: In short, such was the plenty of fish that year, that mackerell, the finest and largest I ever saw, were sold at the sea side a hundred for a penny.

Connected to the Lerret was another traditional small boat, the Trow. Trows are much smaller rowing boats, clinker built like the Lerrets and sometimes built double ended, others

with a small transom. They are flat bottomed, and only draw an inch or two of water, for they are only to be found on the sheltered waters of the Fleet Lagoon, between Chesil Beach and the mainland, where there are extensive mud flats and a shallow draft is essential. They don't have the documentary history of the Lerret, the first mention of a Trow is in a letter of 1815 from a coastguard describing how one was used to catch a smuggler who was ferrying contraband from Chesil Beach to the mainland. However unlike the Lerret which is almost extinct the Trow is still common and anybody walking along the shore of the Fleet can see, at the traditional landing places called Hives (from the old English word for a place where a boat can be beached, as in Hythe, found as the name of the old Kentish port or as part of Rotherhithe), groups of Trows drawn up or bobbing on moorings, just as they have done for centuries.

The Fleet Trows, companion boats to the Lerret, operate exclusively in the Fleet. Unlike many traditional boats Trows are still common and can be found at all the landing places along the shores of the Fleet Lagoon.

Oysters have long been very important to Dorset. Mention has been made of the Roman fisheries. The town of Poole was actually built on the oyster fishery. Under the oldest buildings on the harbour side is a massive deposit of oyster shells. The layer is about a hundred metres long, forty metres wide and over half a metre deep. It contained the remains of between three and seven million oysters!, radiocarbon dating suggesting it was built up over about a hundred and fifty years from the late tenth to the early twelfth centuries. As the town of Poole developed the oyster fishery didn't disappear, it just moved to the edge of the town. By the early eighteenth century:

> This place is famous for the best, and biggest oysters in all this part of England, which the people of Pool pretend to be famous for pickling, and they are barrell'd up here, and sent not only to London, but to the West Indies, and to Spain, and Italy, and other parts. 'Tis observed more pearl are found in the Pool oysters, and larger than in any other oysters about England.

The fishery thrived and by the early nineteenth century:

> A great number of men and boys, obtain a livelihood by their occupation in the fishery, especially by dredging for oysters during the season, the beds of this shell-fish forming their chief resource. The oyster fishery has for many years constituted a lucrative field for the exertions of the fishermen, and its preservation has been an object of great attention to the maritime authorities. Several sloops were laden every year with oysters from thence, which were carried to creeks in the mouth of the River Thames, where they were laid to fatten, to supply the London markets. Forty sloops and boats were employed in this branch of the fishery, for two months every spring, which season was the fishermens' harvest, and during which time they were said to receive upwards of £3000.

The fishery was carefully managed by the town council, who imposed strict regulations on harvesting the oysters:

> [They] fixed the periods between which no oysters should be dredged, limited the number to be taken by each boat, and defined other measures for the promotion and advantage of the fishery.

The busy early twentieth century port of Poole.

This sensible arrangement, which had successfully conserved the fishery was destroyed in 1835 when local councils in England were reformed. The Borough of Poole had opposed the reforms and, almost out of spite, the government refused to let the reformed council of Poole have the management of the oyster fishery.

> It is apprehended that the beds will, in a few years dwindle almost to a state of exhaustion, the wholesome regulations that prevailed for upwards of two hundred years, for restraining the catch according to the state of the beds, having ceased on the abolition of the admiralty jurisdiction.

This led to massive over fishing and the virtual disappearance of the Poole oysters. Happily, fifty years later, the council regained control and immediately imposed fishing licences and regulations, particularly on minimum size, making sure that only mature oysters were caught. The harbour authority continues to control the fishery and Poole oysters can still be enjoyed.

The other oyster fishery is in the Fleet. This has always been privately owned and managed. As early as the eighteenth century oysters were imported to maintain the beds. The fishery has come and gone over the years, but happily survives and local oysters can still be enjoyed in many paces in the county.

Crabs and lobsters have probably always been a part of the local fishing industry. Fragments of crab and lobster shells don't preserve well and are rarely found on archaeological sites, similarly lobster pots wont preserve easily. However by the late seventeenth century a visitor to Swanage noted:

The rectangular frames of the Fleet Oyster Farm are clearly visible from the air.

The old sea pond and jetty at Lulworth Cove. Used to keep lobsters alive before they could be sent to London, or perhaps as an oyster bed.

there I eate y^e best Lobsters and Crabs, being boyled in y^e Sea water and scarce Cold - very large and Sweet.

At this time lobsters were taken from Weymouth to London by horsemen either in panniers behind the saddle or on led horses, and by going as fast as possible they could get there in less than a day.

When they arrive att London, they are neere 3 part dead of them, which are little esteemed of and sold att low prices. With the rest the King's Kitchin is supplied and then the Court and Cittie.

Within a hundred years special 'well boats', were developed, with compartments in the boat full of sea water, and connected to the open sea to keep the water fresh. By this means live lobsters were brought to London from all around the west country. Lobsters were caught and kept alive along the coast in special pools until enough were gathered together to make a cargo. The remains of one of these pools can be seen in Lulworth Cove, behind the curious stone 'quay', its use as a sea pond for lobsters was remembered as recently as the 1930s.

WHALES

Whaling has never been a local trade, though when a whale was washed up on the shore the local people did their best to make a profit out of it. Whales were, and still are, 'Royal Fish', belonging to the king and treated as 'wreck'. If the king had granted the right to a local landowner then he might claim the carcass. Whales were seen as a valuable resource and there could be squabbles, whatever the condition of the beast might be:

1315 Abbotsbury: A certain great fish dead and stinking was on Sunday next after the feast of St Hilary [January 14] in the eighth year of the now King [Edward II] cast by the sea upon the land of the Abbot of Abbotsbury, and Benedict the then Abbot took the same to his own use until John de Erle then Sherriff of the County of Dorset by a writ of the Lord the King took it therefrom to the use of the same the Lord the King to the quantity of two tuns and sent it to London, and no more, because the rest was not good for the use of the Lord the King .

The idea of a wagon load of 'dead and stinking', whale being taken from Abbotsbury to Windsor is pretty revolting. Five hundred years later some people's attitude hadn't changed.

I cannot resist telling you what the late tempestuous weather has produced on the Charmouth Coast, … an animal of such a magnitude, as to strike the beholder with astonishment. On the 5th (February 1840) some of the coast-guard men first discovered the animal near the shore, where it was soon after thrown in by the billows, then alive. I understand great discussion arose as to what was to be done with it, the Lord of the Manor claiming it as his right; in consequence it was cut up piece meal, that he might be benefited, it was supposed from the value of the oil and blubber. It was divided in four and drawn up separately, in a Waggon with four Horses to Mr Bullen's orchard where it continues to be exhibited until tomorrow. It is very much regretted that it should have been so much mangled; if it had remained on the beach and seen in its full size it would have been a much more interesting spectacle. I did not see it until the process of dividing it had commenced, which presented a disgusting spectacle.

The unfortunate Charmouth whale.

If one young woman [quite reasonably] found the sight of a partly dismembered whale a 'disgusting spectacle', others found it less so. After the reassembled corpse had been exhibited (at a penny a head) for a short while, the body was boiled down for the oil. The bones remained as a tourist attraction. Four years later another young woman found the spectacle much less disgusting.

At Charmouth, Jonas Whitcombe [probably Jonas Wishcombe a professional fossilist] used to exhibit the skeleton of a whale which was landed on the beach, and within the ribs of the creature my sister and I used to dance about and run up and down, and play all sorts of pranks. We payed our penny entrance fee and took our money's worth of fun.

If Messrs Bullen and Wishcombe made a profit out of the whale others were not fortunate. The most curious story concerns an unfortunate whale washed up at Boscombe in 1897, on 9th January a 65 foot long whale, weighing an estimated 40 tons, was washed ashore at Pokesdown finally becoming stranded close to Boscombe Pier. It became an instant attraction, as a local newspaper reported:

Below: The bones of an earlier whale form the entrance to a footpath leading to Chideock Manor.

Boys took running jumps up its slippery sides, and tobogganed down them on the seats of their trousers gleefully. Earnest schoolteachers took parties of youngsters and gave lessons in natural history. Farmers poked the thick hide of the beast with sticks, and inland folk raised exclamations of astonishment at its length, its strength and its thickness.

Local children coined a suitable rhyme;

Have you been to Boscombe?
Have you seen the whale?
Have you stood upon its back
And smelt its stinking tail?

The Receiver of Wreck was probably delighted when a local man, Doctor Spencer Simpson purchased the carcass for £27 thinking to make a profit from the blubber.

The Doctor then sought specialist advice as to how to deal with the carcass, and whilst this was happening the smell of the carcass got worse. The Town Clerk, acting for the local Sanitary Authority, irritated by the delay, prosecuted Dr Simpson for causing a nuisance as he hadn't removed the carcass. Despite his claims that he was doing all he could, the court ordered the Doctor to remove the carcass within 48 hours. This was not done and when the Sanitary Inspector, Mr Cooper, came to inspect the rotting whale there was an argument with Doctor Simpson, who, 'drew a swordstick, made a thrust and said he would run him through.' A policeman thought he was going to attack Mr Cooper and took the swordstick. The Sanitary Committee ordered Mr Cooper to lay a complaint, so Dr Simpson appeared in court again and was duly fined £1.

The blubber was then removed and taken in a ketch to the Wytch Channel (well away from anybody who might complain about the smell) whilst Dr Simpson tried to find a buyer. He had valued the blubber at £200 but was only offered 5 shillings. A few months later Dr Simpson found himself in court again, as he hadn't paid the agreed price for the hire of the ketch, he lost again!

Finally the skeleton was cleaned and put on display on Boscombe pier. Dr Simpson tried to recoup his costs by holding a series of lectures on, 'The Wonders of the Deep'. They were not a success, and he hardly made enough to cover the cost of the hall!

The exhibit entranced visitors for several years, particularly young children who would slide down the bones. But, by 1904, the skeleton had begun to crumble and was sold to a local dealer and was ground down to be used in fertiliser.

The skeleton of the Boscombe whale as displayed on Boscombe pier in the early twentieth century.

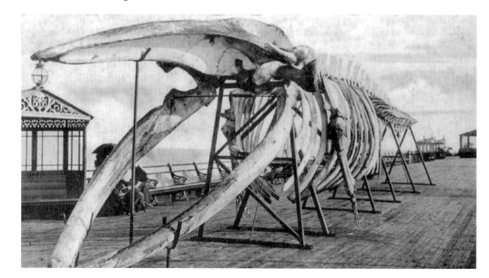

MINERALS
PORTLAND CHERT

The first stone that was used by man, and exported from, the Dorset coast, was Portland chert. This is a very hard grey stone, which occurs in nodules on Portland. It can be worked like flint, and was used from about 8000BC. These Mesolithic people didn't just use the stone, they exported it. In Britain it is found as far west as Cornwall, and as far east as Surrey. As yet it isn't known if the chert was moved by sea, or by land, but sea transport was used at this time. In Christchurch Harbour a small site has been excavated by Mother Siller's Channel, which crosses Stanpit Marsh. Here the hearth was surrounded by large pieces of pieces of Purbeck stone. Whilst it would have been possible to carry the stone by land, it seems rather an unlikely thing to do (it would be a journey of between fifteen and twenty miles), rather the stone was probably brought by water, perhaps as ballast in a skin boat. A similar boat could have easily carried Portland chert along the south coast.

KIMMERIDGE SHALE

In Kimmeridge Bay the cliffs are dark grey and very soft, within these rocks can be found bands of Kimmeridge shale, this is an 'oil shale', so rich in hydrocarbons that it can be burnt, indeed it has sometimes been called 'Kimmeridge Coal'. It can also be polished to a glossy black. In the Bronze age, about 1000 BC it was carved into cups and bowls. The finished vessels, or the raw material, was taken away by sea. There is an amazing piece of evidence that this happened. On of the treasures of the National Museum of Wales is the Caergwrle Bowl. This damaged and incomplete bowl was found in 1823 near Caergwrle Castle in Wales, it is made of Kimmeridge shale and is a model of a boat, and probably quite a big one. It seems from its shape to have been a skin boat, similar to the Irish Curragh, with eyes painted on the bows, probably as a protective charm. Perhaps this type of boat sailed along the Dorset coast three thousand years ago.

Several centuries later the shale was carved into jewellery, particularly bracelets. Rough-outs, in the form of irregular rings of shale, which could be carved into the bracelets, were exported. They have been found in the Iron Age port of Green Island, and even on the sea

Reconstruction drawing of the Caergwyrl Bowl, found in Wales but made of Kimmeridge Shale.

Reconstruction of the Caergwyrl Boat, based on the Caergwyrl Bowl and the large Curraghs (skin covered boats) from Ireland. Did boats like this once sail the coasts of Dorset?

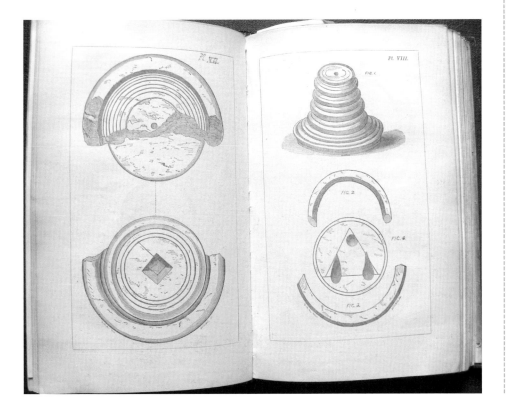

'Kimmeridge Coal Money', are the waste products from the manufacture of Kimmeridge Shale bracelets. These drawings are by John Austen who first realised what coal money really was.

bed near Guernsey. Later, new technology arrived, in the form of the lathe, on which the bracelets were turned. The industry was unaffected by the Roman invasion, indeed it seems that the bracelet makers took advantage of the new markets and shale bracelets can be found all across southern Britain. The Romans made other uses of the shale as trays, table tops and stool legs. However when the Romans left the trade died and was never revived.

In the seventeenth century the shale was used as a fuel, to produce alum and copperas, after the initial experiments:

> Sir William Clavel, who was the owner and Lord of the Manor, took on the works and used the Blackstone [Kimmeridge shale] to heat the furnace. Sir William carried on the works with success, but disaster overtook him just as everything looked most hopeful, when they were seized under the plea that they were an infringement upon a Royal Patent. Nothing daunted, Sir William converted them into a manufactory of glass and salt; he constructed a massive stone-pier to facilitate the removal of the products. All preliminary arrangements were terminated by the action of Sir Robert Mansel, who possessed a Royal Patent which he maintained was infringed upon by Sir William Clavell. When the case was heard before the Privy Council Sir William Clavell was sentenced to imprisonment in the Marshalsea Prison

Local people had used the ashes made from burning the shale as a means of improving clay soil. This attracted the notice of some entrepreneurs in the early nineteenth century who:

> formed the " Bituminous Shale Company," commencing with a capital of £25,000, and having obtained a lease of the cliffs, they erected at Weymouth retorts and other appliances for the manufactory of varnish, paint, lubricating grease, pitch, naphtha, and paraffin.

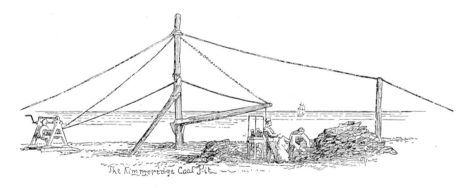

The Kimmeridge Coal Pit

A Kimmeridge 'coal mine', one of the unsuccessful nineteenth century attempts to make a profit from the Kimmeridge Shale

Unfortunately the shale produces foul smelling smoke when burnt, and the company failed in 1854 as it was constantly being fined for polluting the air around Weymouth Quay. Another company now took on the shale, this time treating it in a more isolated plant near Wareham. Although it collected numerous testimonials as to the value of its products, it still couldn't make enough money and after running for four years, it too failed.

The next company thought it had solved the problem, it was going to concentrate on the oil, exporting the shale around the world where it would be distilled and the oil used for lighting. It got the contract for lighting the streets of Paris and began to invest heavily in the Bay. First an iron pier was built, which was quickly replaced by a massive stone pier. The plant near Wareham was enlarged, and all went well for a few years. Then, as usual, the company ran into trouble, money was short and there was still the problem of the smell from the burning shale. The company followed its predecessors into liquidation.

The final attempt to use the shale began in 1876, now the shale would be used to produce 'sanitary carbon', to purify sewerage systems. For some years the company was successful, deeper adits were dug and a light railway built to move the shale to the pier. But the cliffs were unstable, the seam of the shale was narrow and by 1890 the company was loosing money. Mining ceased and for the next sixty years there were no attempts to make money from the geology of Kimmeridge.

Then in 1959 an oil well was dug, which unlike all other ventures at Kimmeridge was successful. At first it produced 350 barrels per day, dropping to 80 barrels in 2009, but it has produced more oil than originally estimated. Finally the geology of Kimmeridge has produced a success story.

PURBECK MARBLE

Purbeck marble is a hard black or dark grey stone which can take a high polish. The Romans had been the first to use it and objects of Purbeck marble have been found across southern Britain. Some were very big, a basin, over a metre across has been found at the legionary fortress at Caerleon, in South Wales. This must have gone by sea, possibly from the quarries in the Purbeck hills down to the Romano-British settlement on Cleavel Point on the shores of Poole Harbour.

A few centuries after the Romans Purbeck marble became the medieval stone of choice for decorative work. It was used extensively for architectural decoration, as it contrasts spectacularly with the light limestones which were frequently used in grand medieval buildings. In Salisbury cathedral there are numerous small columns of Purbeck marble fitted round massive cream columns of Chilmark stone. The other great used of Purbeck marble was for funerary monuments, Purbeck marble grave slabs are frequent and can be found widely across Britain. The commonest type of memorial takes the form of a tapering slab with a raised cross carved on the upper surface. The trade lasted from the late thirteenth to the fifteenth century and was very important to the region. There was a specialist guild, the Purbeck Marblers, who had the right to move their stone from Corfe Castle to the quay at Ower (only a few hundred metres from the Romano-British settlement at Cleavel Point). A late version of the agreement runs:

A Purbeck marble tombstone from Lady St Mary church, Wareham.

A group of Purbeck marble tombstones found in St Edward's Church, Corfe Castle. Corfe was the centre of the marble industry.

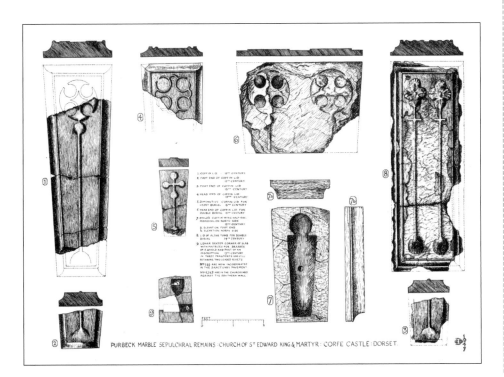

PURBECK MARBLE SEPULCHRAL REMAINS CHURCH OF ST EDWARD KING & MARTYR CORFE CASTLE DORSET.

A coppy of the agreement Between John Collins of Ower and the Quarriers or men called Marblers in the Isle of Purbeck concerning their priviledges at Ower Quay in the Year of Our Lord 1695. To all Christian people whome this shall or may concern this four and Twentieth Day of October 1695. Being an agreement made between John Collins of Ower and the company of Free Marblerrs of Corfe Castle Swanage or others of the Isle of Purbeck and County of Dorset all whome it shall or may concern: For and in consideration of A pound of Pepper and a foot Ball to be paid by the said company of free marblers on the next day following shrove tuesday or in four or five Days after except sabbath day then to be paid the next day following to be paid to the said John Collins his Executors Administrators or Assigns at or in the New Dwelling house of the said John Collins being at Ower abovesaide all which being performed and paid by the free Marblers abovesaid they shall have use occupy and possess the way which was formerly allowed to the said company without any hindrance trouble or molestation of the said John Collins His Heirs or Assigns. The bound of the way being as followeth:- Beginning at said house of John Collins at the Eastside Down along the lane to the strand and so to the Quay. In witness whereof the said John Collins has hereunto set his Hand and seal this Day and Years Above written.

The society of Purbeck Marblers still exists and will pay the landowner at Ower a football and a pound of pepper, whenever it is demanded.

As the trade in Purbeck marble declined the demand for Purbeck stone increased.

PURBECK STONE

As early as the 1720s the Isle of Purbeck was exporting stone, Daniel Defoe noted that:

This part of the country is eminent for vast quarreys of stone, which is cut out flat, and us'd in London in great quantities for paving court-yards, alleys, avenues to houses, kitchins, footways on the sides of the high-streets, and the like; and is very profitable to the place, as also in the number of shipping employed in bringing it to London.

A whim, or small crane, on Portland. Originally used to lower blocks of stone onto boats, they are now used to launch small fishing boats.

All the stone left Purbeck by sea, and unlike the Purbeck marble, this stone wasn't taken to Poole Harbour, it either went to Swanage or was loaded directly onto ships along the coast. Inland quarries tended to send the stone to Swanage, by wagon to the 'bankers', stores of stone close to the shore, then down to shore where it was loaded into a barge, rowed out to a larger sailing vessel and so off.

> We should notice that the stone, from the time it is quarried to the time it at last leaves Swanage, has to be manhandled on five separate occasions: from quarry to wagon, wagon to Banker, Banker to stone cart, stone cart to barge and finally from barge to ocean-going vessel.

However this was not the only way of loading the stone onto the ships. All the way along the coast there are quarries cut into the cliffs. These tend to have flat platforms cut immediately above the sea, from them blocks of stone could be loaded directly into the stone boats. The platforms can be found at the quarries at Hedbury, Seacombe and Winspit, though the largest is at Dancing Ledge. Here the size of the platform may have given it the name, big enough for a ballroom, the ledge also has an unusual feature in the form of a roughly rectangular swimming pool, cut by the masters of Durnford school for the boys to swim in.

It is at Winspit that the whole process can be seen. There is a flat ledge with ruined buildings which housed the old forge which kept the quarrymen's tools in condition. Running back from the ledge are a series of shafts from which the stone was quarried, these are now very dangerous, in several it can be seen that the roof has fallen. The ledges run on either side of a narrow valley that drops down to a lower ledge which is just below high water mark. This ledge is crossed by grooves which form 'rutways', which guided sleds with blocks of stone to the barges. These moored in 'Winspit Dock', a rectangular cut in the stone which enabled barges to come into the little bay and remain there when the tide fell, though

Old Purbeck stone quarries on the hills above Swanage.

Winspit Quarry in the late 1950s. This was the last of the coastal quarries to be worked, though towards the end of its life the stone was removed by lorry rather than stone boats.

Winspit Dock, a rectangular bay cut in the limestone to enable stone boats to float an anchor when the tide fell. The foam at the entrance marks a small rock that would prevent a vessel leaving the dock except at high tide.

no vessel could leave at low water as a large rock, just off shore, would prevent anything leaving. The vessel would have been guided in by posts around the 'dock', their sockets are still clearly visible. The last barge used the dock in 1922. It was nearly a disaster:

> She was towed alongside the cliff and left to load, while her tug put back to Poole. Captain Poulson didn't like the weather. 'Be sure you're back by eleven,' he'd said to the tug skipper; for he knew his laden barge would be helpless if it blew up rough. By midday the loading had been done, and the barge

Rutways, these
grooves cut in the
rock enabled block
of stone, tied to
sleds, to be moved
easily over the rock
ledge.

low and unsteady in the choppy water, wallowed about, a-waiting for her tug.

The sea got up and biggish waves began to lift the barge and smash her against the cliff. We put out fenders and waited, there was little else to do. One o'clock, and there was still no sign of the tug. Two o'clock, and things were looking bad. Three o'clock and she was filling fast, we set to work on the pumps but the pump-handle was rusted almost through and soon brought off. Then, steaming towards us in a great squall of rain, we saw the tug: five hours late. They were just in time to save us, another half hour and we would have been drowned.

But the really surprising thing at Winspit are the carvings, a unique record of the ships that sailed past the quarry and took the stone to London and beyond.

The ships illustrated fall into one of two categories, fore and aft rigged sailing barges or square-riggers. The majority of the carvings of the sailing barges represent single masted sailing vessels. Most appear to be gaff rigged, that is where the upper edge of the main sail is supported along its entire length by a spar, the gaff. In addition there are four drawings

Ship graffiti. A unique feature of the Winspit quarries, these carvings were made by the quarrymen and show the ships which carried the stone from the Isle of Purbeck to the wider world.

Portland Castle. Although built nearly five hundred years ago the stone is still sharp cut, a testament to the quality of Portland stone as a building material.

of two masted vessels with fore and aft rig. These all seem to have a marked difference in the height of the two masts.

There are also three square-rigged ships illustrated in the graffiti, two rather eroded. The best preserved shows a two masted vessel, with sails set on the main mast and furled on the fore. The other square rigged ships are much less clear but they both have at least three masts, and numerous yards. The large number of yards is reminiscent of the massive sailing vessels of the latter half of the nineteenth century, best exemplified by the famous clipper ships.

Most of the ships portrayed are of the types shown in contemporary illustrations of the Purbeck stone trade. They seem to have been cut with a chisel or punch, and it is reasonable to assume that they were cut by quarrymen, who certainly would have had the skill, and the tools, to make the carvings. Indeed, the position of many of the carvings, at the entrances of some of the galleries, would be consistent with this suggestion. None of the galleries were particularly deep, and when the quarrymen stopped work for lunch they almost certainly walked to the end of the gallery to have their meal, which is just where the graffiti were cut.

It certainly makes a pleasing picture, the quarryman, having eaten his meal takes a short rest before returning to his labour. As he rests he carves a picture of a boat, one of those he sees every day as they carry their load of stone from the quarries to Swanage or beyond.

PORTLAND STONE

Portland stone is one of the finest building stones on the world. It was used locally for many years, then in the early sixteenth century it was used for Portland Castle; this is the oldest extant building in the stone and its quality is clear, after nearly five hundred years the cut edges are still sharp. In 1619 work started on the Banqueting House at Whitehall. This building, designed by the great architect Inigo Jones, was the first major building built in Portland stone away from the island. It began a link between Portland and the city of London which has endured for centuries, as Daniel Defoe wrote in 1724:

Hence it is, that our best and whitest free stone comes, with which the cathedral of St Paul's, the Monument, and all the publick edifices in the city

of London, are chiefly built; and 'tis wonderful, and well worth the
observation of a traveller to see the quarries in the rocks, from whence they
are cut out, what stones, and of what prodigious a size are cut out there.

The stone was moved by ships, from a series of little piers along the coast, King's Pier,
Duddle Pier, Folly Pier. Here the stone would be loaded
into small sailing vessels. At the beginning of the twenty-
first century a remarkable find was made in Weymouth
Bay, the wreck of an eighteenth century sailing vessel
carrying Portland stone.

Portland in 1811,
the various stone
piers on the east
coast of the island
are clearly marked.

The vessel was over 25 metres long and carried a cargo
of approximately 65 to 75 tons of cut Portland stone,
which ranged in size from the biggest at 6 foot by 3 foot
by 2 foot 9 inches, weighing an estimated 3.36 tonnes
down to a block weighing just 67 kg and measuring 1 foot
9 inches by 9 inches by 9 inches. The blocks had been
roughly shaped, in some cases into segments of arches, to
lighten the load as much as possible. The stone was
probably on its way to London where the stone would
receive its fine carving before being used in a grand
building. The wreck was dated from the single coin found,
a halfpenny of 1721, and it was interesting to find shot
from a 24 bore carbine, presumably on board to protect
the boat from French privateers.

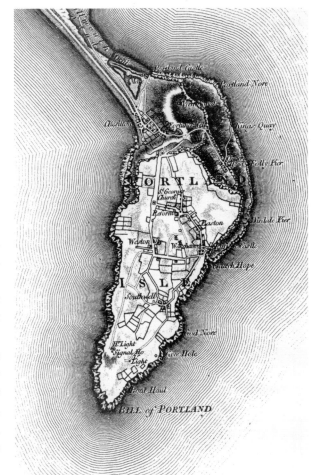

The minor piers round the edge of the island fell out
of use in the nineteenth century as the railway began to
take more and more stone away, though it continued to be
loaded onto vessels at Castle Pier, by Portland Castle, until
well into the twentieth century. The last stone boat, a
commemorative one, sailed in 1972. The era of the stone
boats was over.

CHESIL BEACH

Chesil Beach is one of the largest masses of shingle in Britain, and it is hardly surprising that for many years it was quarried for gravel. In the 1950s its export was virtually the only trade left for Bridport Harbour.

> "It is the only the only trade left to us now."
> "And do you dig gravel from any part of the beach?" I asked him.
> "Good heavens no! Only two or three miles of the Chesil Bank have gravel of the right grade; three-eights of an inch that is. It's dug by hand, high up on the beach, and loaded into lorries. Lower down, by the water's edge, they dig sand, and that's loaded into carts. Most of it goes to Scotland in gravel barges of 250 to 380 tons, and a few cargoes find their way to Manchester or Sunderland,"

The export by boats stopped shortly afterwards, though it was twenty years before the damaging trade of exporting the shingle was stopped.

Once the shingle of Chesil Beach was quarried for gravel, now it is protected as its importance to the protection of the coast has been realised.

3: Travelling and Trading

THERE ARE A NUMBER OF PORTS along the Dorset coast, ranging from large to small, successful to failures. There are stories of amazing success, to almost tragic failures and in one case the port has vanished and no one knows exactly where it was. The ports of Dorset were the places where men looked outwards and the history of the ports is the history of Dorset's relations with the rest of the world.

LYME REGIS

The story of Lyme Regis as a port is the story of one of the most remarkable buildings of medieval Dorset – the Cobb. The Cobb is so well known that it is sometimes difficult to realise how remarkable it is. When it was first built stone piers like this were extremely rare, many sailors who visited when the Cobb was new, or indeed during the first three hundred years of its existence, will never have seen anything so elaborate in the rest of their sailing lives.

It is unknown when the Cobb was first built. The first mention is in a grant dated 1313 from King Edward III, of part of the revenues of the port towards repairing the Cobb, which had been damaged by storms. Clearly it had been built some years earlier, in the thirteenth century, possibly in the reign of Edward I, when the town was made a free borough. The document states that the Cobb was built of wood and rocks (*maeremio et petris*).

The harbour at Lyme Regis, surrounded by the Cobb, one of the most remarkable medieval building in Dorset.

The foundations of the Cobb, set in a natural ridge of rock, as recorded by Major Fanshaw in 1818, during his first restoration of the Cobb.

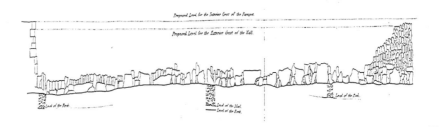

This description would fit the Cobb as shown on the earliest known drawing. A curving wall, not linked to the shore, with vertical timber sides, packed full of large stones. When the Cobb was badly damaged by storms in the early nineteenth century the original base of the Cobb could be seen:

> I perceived at the repair of the Cobb in 1825, that some part of it was built of piles once unprotected by a wall. They were in three rows, and were supported by large rocks. They were just inside the outer line of the wall, which was, after they were found insufficient, built over them.

It was rebuilt again in 1329 and 1376 after very serious damaged by storms. But even ordinary high winds could damage it and it required constant maintenance. At the end of the sixteenth century Thomas Gerard noted that:

The Tudor Cobb, a stone and timber structure set some way away from the town of Lyme Regis. This plan dates from about 1536.

> The town flourisheth, well built, and enriched by the Conveniencie of the Cobb, which is an Harbour that the Inhabitants, with much Industrie and Charge, have built in the sea, by pileing together great Rocks, which at low water with empty Caskes they weigh up, and by this Meanes have made the Harbour safe for Barkes of good Burthen to ride in : For the better repaireing and enlargeing of which, they choose yearly two Overseers, whom they call Cobwardens, whose office is to see the Cobb well repaired of those Breaches, which manie times the Sea makes in it.

A hundred years later nothing much had changed:

> The Cob at Lyme, a small port in Dorsetshire, that is situate in the [bottom] of a bay where there is no river or land-lock, provided by nature to prevent the certain loss of ships at anchor there; and of all places upon the coast of England, least to be suspected for a good port. But art and industry will do wonders; for all the requisites of a safe harbour are supplied by this Cob. The Cob is a mole built in the sea, about two furlongs from the town, and named from the cobble-stone of which it is compiled. There is not any one like it in the whole of England.

During the eighteenth century the Cobb was gradually rebuilt in mortared masonry. The importance of the harbour to the nation, as the only safe refuge for ships on an otherwise very dangerous coast, meant that the government was prepared to pay for the maintenance of the repair of the wall whenever it was badly damaged. In 1792 the southern pier was swept away, and was repaired by Captain D'Arcy of the Ordnance Board. The government seems to have thought that it took the same skills in building fortifications to provide protection from cannon fire as it did in building walls to protect from the power of the sea. At Lyme the government was proved right!

Captain D'Arcy's work still stands, a worn inscription records details of his work.

> The work extending 273 feet west of this stone was erected by James Hamilton, builder and contractor with the honourable Board of Ordnance, to repair the breaches made in the Cobb in January, 1792, under the direction of Captain D'Arcy, engineer, 1795.

The inscription recording the restoration of the outer pier in 1795 by Captain D'Arcy.

But the greatest hero in Lyme's long battle with the sea was Captain Fanshaw. In 1818 he had come to Lyme Regis to repair a short section of the Cobb where the pier curves halfway along its length. In 1824 the Cobb had been devastated by a terrible storm:

> All the old work, between the new work to near the Gin-shop, in length 232 feet, was thrown down; the northern wall, the Crab-head, and the quay, were much injured, and a scene of devastation was presented that defies description. Persons ran about, after seeing the ruin at low water, exclaiming that Lyme was ruined, and that the injuries could never be repaired.

But the repairs of Captain Fanshaw, six years earlier had stood firm. There was an immediate call in the town for him to return to rebuild the devastated harbour. The government granted their wish and Colonel Fanshaw returned. His work was a triumph, at the end a plaque was erected in the 'Gin Shop' a small recess in the middle of the Cobb where a small crane or en-GIN-e was kept:

The harbour at Lyme
Regis, in about
1950.

The harbour at Lyme
Regis, in about
1950.

The plaque in the
Gin Shop,
commemorating the
fact that Colonel
Fanshaw restored the
main pier at less than
the estimated cost.

BY ORDER OF
THE MASTER GENERAL AND BOARD OF ORDNANCE

The repair of this Cobb was commenced and finished under the direction of
Lieut-Col. Fanshaw, Royal Engineers, by order of the Master General, dated
April 2nd, 1825, and under the immediate superintendence of Captain
Savage of the same corps.

Length of pier rebuilt, 232 feet
Length of parapet rebuilt, 447 feet
Amount of estimate £19,193 19s. 10d.
Amount of expenditure £17,337 0s. 9¼d
Date of commencement of the work 19th April, 1825.
Date of completion of the work, 18th November, 1825.

Then as now it was considered amazing that a major public work like this could be brought
in under budget!

Colonel Fanshaw was clearly a brilliant engineer, for his work has stood firm and
protected Lyme Regis from whatever the sea could throw against it, for over one hundred
and seventy years!

With the safety of the Cobb behind them, the men of Lyme Regis were able to take part
in the burgeoning international trade of the sixteenth and seventeenth centuries.

> It appears by the old custom-house papers that [during the reign of James I]
> a lucrative trade was carried on with Guinea, from which were imported the
> usual commodities of elephants teeth and gold dust. The duties paid to the
> government from Lyme were very considerable: during the latter part of
> James's reign, they amounted some years to more that £5000 per annum.

It seems amazing now, but Lyme Regis was a fairly major player in the developing trade with
the African Coast. Each port tended to look to one part of the world when it came to
international trading, Poole to North America, in particular Newfoundland, Weymouth to
continental Europe and the Mediterranean, and Lyme Regis – Africa. The first trading
venture was in the barque *Cherubim*, to Senegal and the Gambia as early as 1591. Over the
next few years this trade developed – it declined after about 1610, but resumed at the end

of the century. Ships would leave for the African coast in the summer with cargos of cloth, and metal goods, not just the traditional cooking pots but also musical instruments, trumpets and bugles were particularly popular. Returning about a year later, to paraphrase John Masefield

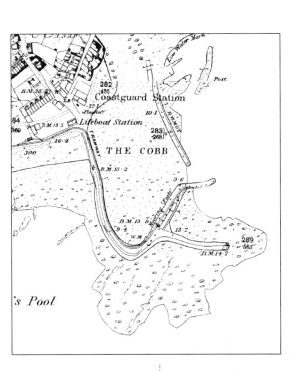

With a cargo of ivory, and gold moidores.

To give a few examples:

The *Princess*, left Lyme on 22 August 1720, and returned from Guinea on 16 October 1721 with a cargo of 67 cwt, 1 qtr, 11 lb of elephants teeth and 17 tons, 14 cwt, 2 qtr, 21 lb of redwood (plant material used as a dye)

The following year she left Lyme on 17 June 1722, and returned from Guinea on 2 August 1723 with a cargo of, 58 cwt, 2 qtr of elephants teeth and 18 tons, 14 cwt, 1 qtr, 16 lb of redwood (dyestuff)

The Cobb in 1886, it is now virtually in its present form.

When eighteenth century commerce with Africa is mentioned, people tend to think of the slave trade, forgetting this two way trade, which was advocated by anti-slavery campaigners like Thomas Clarkson. Manufactured goods going out and local produce coming back, truly a respectable trade.

Over the past few years divers have found a number of elephants' tusks on the sea bed between Portland and West Bay. These are all from African plains elephants and are clearly not fossils. In 2005, a number of these tusks were brought together at Weymouth Museum, and for the first time in 300 years it was possible to see what a ship like the *Princess* might have been bringing home. It is likely that these tusks were from a sister-ship of the *Princess*, and brings home the uncertainties of a sailor's life at this time. The ship had been away from home, for nearly a year. It had visited an area notoriously unhealthy to Europeans, the contemporary rhyme summed it up:

Beware, beware the Bight of the Benin, for few come out though many go in.

Some of the crew would probably have died from fevers, and now, with Portland to starboard, Golden Cap on the horizon, a day's sail from home, she goes down. That is bad luck, that was too often a sailors fate.

Elephant's tusk from Lyme Bay, possibly lost from one of the ships which traded from Lyme Regis to Africa in the early eighteenth century.

A 'Parcel of elephants' teeth', as they were described in the customs documents on the eighteenth century. Many of the known elephants' tusks recovered from Lyme Bay were brought together at Weymouth Museum for a temporary exhibition.

As the eighteenth century progressed the ships that sailed for Africa grew too big for the Cobb to handle. The Africa merchants in Lyme transferred their business to London or Bristol and the Cobb settled down to handle the coastal trade. Of these small ships the most famous is the *Unity*, whose story is intimately connected with that of the great storm of 1824.

The railway came to Lyme in 1896, and virtually killed off this trade. The last commercial vessel to offload cargo onto the Cobb sailed in 1932, since when Lyme Regis has served fishermen and pleasure craft, and served them very well.

BRIDPORT

The story of Bridport Harbour is a strange and rather sad one. For centuries men have looked at the mouth of the Brit and thought, along with the early Tudor traveller John Leland that:

> Nature hath so set this Ryver Mouth in a Valley bytwixt 2 Hilles that with cost the Sea might be brought in, and [there an Haven] made.

However tempting it might be, his near contemporary William Camden noted that:

> Neither is this place able to maintaine the name of an haven, albeit in the mouth of the river, being enclosed on both sides enclosed within little hilles, nature seemes as it were of purpose to have begun an haven, and requireth in some sort art and mans helpe to accomplish the same.

For centuries the men of Bridport tried to build a harbour and when, at last, they succeeded they had only a few years of profitable trading before increasing ship size rendered it useless.

The town of Bridport has long been associated with the manufacture of ropes. As early as 1213 King John ordered that the rope makers worked night and day if necessary to get the cordage ready for his navy, and in 1225 Henry III directed the sheriff to buy two cables in the town and send them to Fowey for the use of the royal ships. Rope making continued to be important to the town, indeed nets are still made there. This led to the macabre saying:

> To be stabbed with a Bridport Dagger.

Meaning to be hung, though at least one traveller noted that Bridport was famous for making daggers! Perhaps the locals were having fun with him.

At this time ships would probably sail up the Brit and off load close to the town. This is born out by the earliest direct references to a harbour. In 1274 the men of Bridport complained that:

> The abbot of Cernel [Cerne Abbas] and the prior of Fromton [Frampton] take all wreck coming from the sea between two cliffs on each side of the sluice, belonging to the borough of Bridport, by what authority they know not. And they say that the prior aforesaid does not allow the burgesses to take tolls in the harbour (portus) belonging to the borough which they were accustomed and ought to take, nor had he allowed them for sixteen years past, to the damage of the borough of half-a mark (6s. 8d.) yearly.

The Prior of Frampton responded saying he had done nothing wrong:

> The jury present that there is a certain stream of fresh water which reaches
> to the sea, in which boats come to land (applico) as far as the borough of
> Brideport, and there they were accustomed to take for each boat coming to
> land at that place one penny, until Alveredus the prior of Frompton during
> all his time took the said penny to the damage of our lord the King of half
> a mark yearly. And the prior comes and says that the aforesaid toll belongs
> to him and that he takes nothing unless it is his and upon his land. He asks
> for an enquiry.

This suggests that the landing place was up the river, with only slight structures at the river mouth.

On the outskirts of Bridport there is an unusual medieval building that may be associated with this harbour. This is the Chantry which was built in the late thirteenth or early fourteenth century. It is a prominent two storey medieval building on the western side of South Street, and has been traditionally associated with the harbour.

It is uncertain how the court case ended, however by 1385 the town had complete control of the harbour, since in that year work started to construct a harbour on the shore. By 1393 the harbour was complete, but it didn't last long. It may have been damaged by French raids, certainly within fifty years it was it was in a ruinous condition, and the men of Bridport were too poor to restore it. In 1447 they received indulgences from the Archbishops of Canterbury and York as well as thirteen other bishops. Indulgences were a popular means of late medieval fund raising. The church promised that, by purchasing an indulgence, the buyer's soul would not have to spend too long in purgatory. The sale of indulgences was one of the activities of the Roman Catholic church which so incensed Martin Luther and led to the Protestant Reformation. Bridport was unlucky, the indulgences were not at all popular, and one of the collectors wrote that to his 'great shame and anger' he was not making enough to pay his expenses, whilst another vanished with all that he had received. The late medieval harbour of Bridport disappeared.

By 1565 a report noticed that:

> There is one landing place called Bridport mouth, being one mile distant
> from the town of Bridport. There is no harbour at the said landing place,
> neither can any stay or discharge there, but such as may with an engine called
> a capstone and force of men be drawn upon the land.

A Dorset beach capstan, the only provision for visiting merchantman at Bridport Harbour in the sixteenth century.

In 1619 work started again on the harbour, more collections were made, this time from parishes across the south of England. The parish register of Preshute in Wiltshire records that during morning prayers:

> A collection for ye towne of Bridport in ye county of Dorset for ye repayring of a haven nere adjoyning to ye said towne called Bridport Mouth w'ch was ye only means yt enriched ye said towne.

Enough money was collected to repair the capstan but loading and unloading was only possible from beached vessels. There was still no harbour.

In the seventeenth century a new method of fundraising for such projects had been developed, an Act of Parliament. This would allow the town council to borrow money for building the harbour and repaying the loans from the expected profits. The first attempt to get an act was in 1701, but this failed as lenders were not willing to make loans for rebuilding the harbour, which was not at all surprising in the light of earlier history. The town made another attempt in 1721 and this occasion were rewarded by success, and Bridport was for the first time empowered to buy the land and the raise the necessary capital by means of loans to be repaid by tolls levied on ships and cargoes using the harbour. Despite this there was still the matter of actually raising the money and it was not until 1740 that work started.

Two piers were built and the course of the River Brit was diverted to run between them. A sluice gate was built at the mouth of the river to control the flow of water into the harbour so that:

> After completion the harbour shall be so scoured by the pent-up water that at least eleven feet of water shall be between the piers at all springtides, so that vessels of 100 tons shall safely enter or leave the harbour at such times without hindrance from any bar of sand.

The harbour dues gradually rose from £18 in 1743 (when the harbour reopened) to £800 thirty years later. Storms took their toll, repairs were needed within three years, but the profits were such that work soon started on building the harbour basin and lining it with stone walls. By the beginning of the nineteenth century it had become clear that the piers of 1740 were no longer sufficient Between 1807 and 1818 the wooden piers were almost completely rebuilt and extended. Despite all these problems Bridport finally had its harbour.

Bridport Haven has long been barred up by the tides with sand, but after many fruitless attempts to restore it, here is a safe port where may ride about 40 sail.

Bridport Harbour as planned by Lt Murdoch Mackenzie in 1787, the wooden piers finally provided a safe anchorage for shipping.

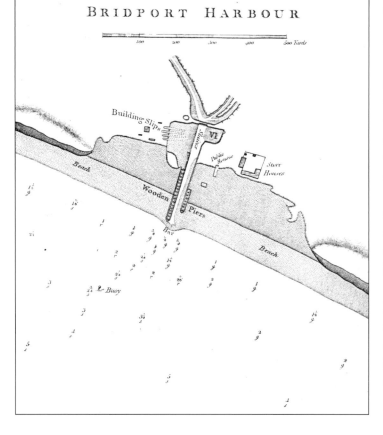

With expanding trade after the Napoleonic War the town council decided to completely rebuild the harbour. In 1823 a new Act of Parliament was obtained setting up the harbour under a body of statutory commissioners. A new basin was dug and lined with stone, the piers were rebuilt, first again in wood, then in 1866, in stone, a new road was built from the harbour to Bridport. The number of ships visiting doubled in three years and in 1832 Bridport became a 'bond-port,' with its own Customs House. This was the high point of Bridport Harbour, and it lasted less than a generation. The railway reached Bridport in 1857 and soon the goods that had been sent out by sea were leaving by rail, other trade diminishing as wooden sailing vessels were replaced by iron steam ships. In 1881 there was so little trade that Bridport Harbour lost its status as a bond-port and in 1884 its name! The Great Western Railway built a branch line to the harbour and, realising that their best hope of profit was to market the harbour as a holiday resort called the station, 'West Bay', as being more appealing to the prospective holiday maker. West Bay stuck and the name Bridport Harbour has almost been forgotten.

Bay House (left) and the Nunnery at Dunster (right). Bay House was built in 1885 as a hotel for what was hoped to be a new holiday resort. The design of the building deliberately copied a medieval house at Dunster in Somerset, so it cold claim to be a 'local design'. As with most schemes connected with Bridport Harbour the holiday resort idea also failed.

WEYMOUTH

Weymouth has a surprisingly complex history, the earliest port wasn't anywhere near the present harbour but several miles up the valley at Radipole. Now inland, the damp meadows below the church were once a tidal inlet and behind the present church the Roman port stood. Not only are there traces of buildings here but, in the nineteenth century a Roman amphora was found in Weymouth Backwater, dropped from a vessel going in or out of the port of Radipole. Sadly very little is known about the port, when it began and when it was abandoned. It could have been an Iron Age port like those at Poole and Christchurch, serving the massive hill fort of Maiden Castle. It may have continued after the Romans left, like the town of Wareham. These are questions only archaeology can answer, one day perhaps.

The first mention of Weymouth is in a grant of King Athelstan, in 938, where he gives to Milton Abbey of:

> All that Water within the shore of Waymuth, and half the stream of that
> Waymuth out at sea twelve acres for the support of the wear and its officer,
> three Thanes and a saltern by the were, and sixty seven hides of land in its
> neighbourhood.

Unlike Lyme Regis there is plenty of space in the broad estuary of the Wey for a saltern, though where it was is unknown.

It was somewhere around the year 1000 that people from the villages of Wyke Regis and Radipole moved to the site of present day Weymouth and created two, separate ports.

Weymouth, on the southern side of the estuary was part of Wyke Regis, whilst Melcombe Regis on the northern side was part of Radipole.

In about 1110 King Henry I granted, to the Prior and Monks of St Swithin and Winchester:

> The ports of Waimuth and Melecumb, with all its appurtenances, together with the manors of Wike and Portelond, which king Edward gave them, and that they might enjoy all the liberties, wrecks, and all free customs, by sea and by land, as they had ever enjoyed them.

This is the first mention of the a port, or rather ports, at Weymouth and Melcombe Regis. The two separate ports both became boroughs, Weymouth in 1252 and Melcombe Regis in 1280. They both prospered, particularly with cross channel trade – their merchants traded to France for wine, to Spain for oil and to Norway for furs. In 1310 Melcombe became a staple port for wool. All was set for a prosperous future, then:

> In the year of the Lord 1348, about the feast of the translation of St. Thomas [July 7] the cruel pestilence, terrible to all future ages, came from parts over the sea to the south coast of England, into a port called Melcombe, in Dorsetshire. This [plague] sweeping over the southern districts, destroyed numberless people in Dorset, Devon and Somerset.

and

> In this year, 1348, in Melcombe in the county of Dorset, a little before the feast of St John the Baptist [June 24], two ships, one of them from Bristol, came alongside. One of the sailors had brought with him from Gascony the seeds of the terrible pestilence, and through him the men of that town of Melcombe were the first in England to be infected.

The Black Death, as it was later called, killed between a third and a half of the population of Britain. Melcombe and Weymouth were badly hit, and this was only the beginning of the problems the ports faced. As the French wars progressed the two towns were easy targets. In 1386:

> The French King on his parte greatly fortified his navy, they did great damage to the realm of England, there was none that could sail out of England, but they were robbed, slain, or taken, and one Sunday, they came in the forenoon, to the haven of Melcombe, while the people were at mass, and the Normans, Genoese, Bretons, Picards, and Spaniards, entered into the town and robbed and pillaged the town, and slew many, and defiled maidens, and enforced [raped] wives, and loaded their vessels with that pillage, and so entered again into their ships, and when the tide came they up-anchored and sailed to Normandy, and came to Dieppe, and there departed and divided their booty.

Again and again at this time the towns appealed to the king claiming that they were unable to pay their taxes due to the damage caused by French raids. In 1433 Melcombe lost its position as a

The list of incumbents from the church at Winterborne Houghton. The church had four different priests during the years 1348-9, some of them were probably victims of the Black Death.

staple port to Poole since it could no longer handle the trade. But as one avenue closed another opened. In 1428 licences were granted to various ports of England, to act as the departure points for pilgrims going to the famous shrine of St James at Compostela in Spain. Weymouth and Melcombe were granted this privilege and soon became the third most important port for pilgrims after London and Bristol.

A list of some of the ships involved in the pilgrim trade survives:

> Ye Katherine, Ye Galliotte, Ye Marye Batte, Ye Little Nicholas, Ye Pylgryme, Ye Holye Ghoste, Ye Saynte Marye, Ye Adventrer, Ye Dorcette

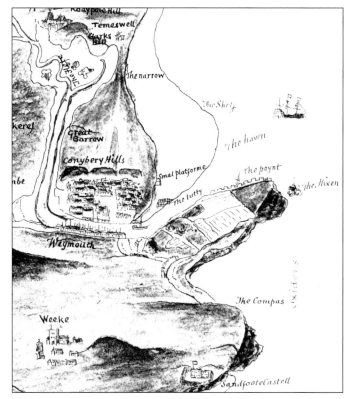

A Tudor map of Weymouth and Melcombe Regis before the bridge was built.

And in 1466, James Butler, Earl of Wiltshire had licence to visit the shrine of St James of Compostela, with thirty persons in his suite, "yn ye shyppe caullid ye Sanyte Iago of Waymuthe". Clearly these vessels were built for the trade as several of them seem to have names linked to the trade, *Holy Ghost, Saint Mary, Saint James* (Iago) and *Pilgrim*.

Developing trade and increasing wealth led to another problem. Weymouth and Melcombe Regis were separate towns with separate governments, rivalry soon dominated the relations between the towns. As William Camden said:

> The Ryver Way, passing thence, names little villages, and then falls into the sea at Waymouth, opposite to which, on the other banke, stands Melcombe, an ancient borough, between whom and Waymonth arose great controversy, both enjoying like privelages, and both challenging the particular immunities of the Haven, which lyeth in the very bosom of them; each of them have taken the overthrow of the other: but not resting by that, continually commenced new suits.
>
> At length having wearied the lords of the council and other courts with their contentious importunities, by the advice of that wise counsellor, William Cecil, lord treasurer of England, they were by an act of parliament incorporated in one bodye, governed by one mayor, and aldermen, his assistants.

The seal of Melcombe Regis.

The seal of the united boroughs of Weymouth and Melcombe Regis.

Elizabeth's charter of 1571 formally united the two towns, which would henceforth be called the borough of Weymouth and Melcombe Regis (officially it still is). However uniting the councils didn't end the rivalry, there are constant complaints of, for example a constable from Weymouth being prevented from arresting someone in Melcombe, or the men of Weymouth refusing to recognise the appointment of the Mayor just because he happened to come from Melcombe. It took a physical act to unite the towns. At this time the only way to cross between the towns was by ferry, as John Leland said:

> The Tounlet of Waymouth lyith strait agayn Milton on the other side of the haven, and at this place, the Trajectus [ferry] is by a bote and a rope, bent over the haven, so that yn the fery-bote they use no ores.

This was slow and inefficient and in 1597 a bridge was built, not by the people of Weymouth or Melcombe Regis but by a group of London merchants who were as exasperated as the government had been by the constant bickering between the two towns. It was this that finally led to the end of the rivalry.

> These stood both sometime proudlie upon their owne several privelidges and were in emulation one of the other, but now tho (God turne it to the good of both,) many, they are, by authoritie of parliament, incorporated into one bodie, conjoyned by late by a bridge and growne very much greetier and goodlier in buildings, and by sea adventures than heretofore.

These sea adventures now included trans Atlantic trade. In 1583 Richard Clark, 'captain and pilot of Weymouth' had sailed with Sir Humphrey Gilbert on his voyage which cemented England's control of Newfoundland. Weymouth was an early player in the Newfoundland Trade, sending up to forty ships a year. These links with America helped the Puritan clergyman John White of Dorchester who established the Dorchester Company in 1624, an enterprise aimed at creating a 'godly colony in America'. The Dorchester Company was, eventually, successful becoming part of the Massachusetts Bay Company. In the first half of the seventeenth century, as well as ships bound for Newfoundland for the fishing

The Victorian Weymouth Bridge with a swinging central section.

The new Weymouth Bridge of 1930, just after it was completed.

were ships carrying colonists who were to establish towns such as Salem, or notable early colonial administrators such as John Endicott who helped protect the young settlements during the political chaos of the commonwealth and restoration.

Two hundred years earlier the town had lost its position as the principal customs port to the town of Poole, now it was to lose its trade with Newfoundland. In 1622 the mayor of Weymouth complained that in that year only 11 ships had been sent to the fishery instead of 39 as before. The Civil War dealt another blow to the port. Weymouth was the centre of a great deal of fighting and changed hands several times, as a result the harbour walls and sea defences were neglected and the American traders left Weymouth never to return. In 1708, fifty years after the end of the war, the harbour was ' choked up with sand occasioned by the ruins of the said quays and bridge,' so that only the smallest vessels could enter instead of those of 200 or 300 tons as formerly.

> Melcombe and Weymouth were formerly in a very flourishing state, yet the great poverty brought upon the town by the Newfoundland trade being taken away, the injury received during the civil wars, by fires irruptions of the French, the neglect of public spirit, private animosities, engendered by feuds among the corporate body, etc., all combined together to render the towns the scene of desolation and poverty: about the beginning of the last century [1700] it was in a truly deplorable condition, and scarcely any idea can be formed of the general devastation and depression that every where prevailed; houses were of little value, and purchasers could scarcely be procured at any rate; the streets were deserted, and those tenements which in times by gone, were wont to be the scene of mirth and revelry, then, the lonely step of the wanderer, scared from their concealment, the owls, bats, and other midnight prowlers; the population had dwindled to a mere nothing, and indeed no person could venture to patrol the streets, without being in imminent danger of burying their bones among a mouldering heap of dust; the rolling wheel of a carriage proved a source of intense attraction, the shipping had dwindled to a mere nonentity, commerce and trade had disappeared, and when the wants of the few inhabitants required any replenishment, they were obliged to procure them from the county town: as the old tenements fell down.

Perhaps a bit exaggerated, but there is no doubt that by the middle of the eighteenth century Weymouth was no longer a major port. There was local trade and some trade with France and Spain, but to an observer of the time Weymouth would have seemed to be a port on the way out, liable to shrink to a fishing village. Two things were to save Weymouth, tourism and steam. Tourism, beginning in the middle of the eighteenth century, bought prosperity to the town. As a contemporary writer noted

> This influx of visitors completely put the inhabitants, who had been retrograding, on the "qui vive," a stimulus was given to building, commerce once more resumed her station at this port, industry applied itself to erect edifices, suitable for the residences of the noble and the opulent; a strong wall enclosing a great deal of what was once sand and sea, was erected, and the space thus taken from the Bay, was converted into a beautiful semicircular marine walk, of thirty feet wide, and one mile in length, called the Esplanade; speculation was afloat, and the natives at last began to think, that the rear of their houses should be converted into their front; land which before was considered not worth enclosing, was now anxiously sought after, and whole

rows of handsome and beautiful houses were erected, which have since been considerably increased in number and size, on spots hitherto, where the browsing kine chewed the cud, or Neptune with his trident and train of Tritons, sportively rode on the bosom of the rolling surges; the natural influx of wealth, produced wants, which were before unknown here.

This time the comments aren't exaggerated, with renewed interest in Weymouth as a place, its proximity to the Channel Islands was noticed officially and in 1794 Weymouth became the base for the Channel Island Packet boats, carrying mail to the islands. In 1827 the first steam vessel carried the mail from Weymouth to Guernsey. The speed of the *Watersprite* amazed contemporary writers:

> On Wednesday last, two gentleman having taken their breakfast in London, departed by the Magnet coach and arrived at the Golden Lion, Weymouth, the same evening, in good time for the packet so that on the following morning they were seated at their breakfast at Payns Hotel, Gurnsey, all accomplished within 24 hours.

The wreck of the *Meteor* on Portland. The artist has clearly never been anywhere near the island!

In 1830 the steam packet *Meteor* gained the dubious honour of being the first steam vessel to be wrecked on the Dorset coast. Trying to get into Weymouth in fog she ran onto rocks near Church Ope on Portland. All the passengers and crew were saved, as was the mail, although the Portlanders behaved traditionally by stealing the passengers' luggage from the wrecked vessel.

Apart from a few years when the service moved to Poole (after the railway had reached Poole but before it reached Weymouth), the link to the Channel Islands has remained ever since. The trade with the islands was also important; the importation of fruit and vegetables was as valuable to the islands as to Weymouth. Of all the various vessels that have served on this route none is more famous than the *St Helier*.

As her name suggests she was built for the Channel Island trade in 1925 and served successfully on the route until 1939 when she was taken into government service. Her war record was remarkable. In May 1940 she was ordered to Dunkirk! In the words of J B Priestley, who was describing another requisitioned vessel that made the journey to the beaches:

Weymouth Harbour from the Nothe in about 1950. The heroic channel steamer *St Helier* is moored on the far side.

This little steamer, like all her brave and battered sisters, is immortal. She will go sailing down the years in the epic of Dunkirk. And our great-grandchildren, when they learn how we began this War by snatching glory out of defeat, and then swept on to victory, may also learn how the little holiday steamers made an excursion to hell and came back glorious

The *St Helier's* 'excursion to hell', involved one trip to Calais and seven trips to Dunkirk during which she rescued 1500 refugees and 10200 troops. Four years later she returned to France, carrying Canadian soldiers to Juno Beach on D Day. A gallant little steamer indeed.

After the Second World War the general trade of the harbour declined, leaving just the Channel Island ferries and pleasure craft. But the harbour is still busy, if only an echo of its former life.

THE PORTS OF POOLE HARBOUR

It is a curious phenomenon that a port will move over time. It has been noticed on many occasions that, if the local geography will allow, the centre of trading activities in a port will move, sometimes only over a short distance, but on other occasions over several miles.

The most remarkable example of this phenomenon can be found around the shore of Poole Harbour. The ports of Poole have probably moved the most of any port or ports in the world. From the prehistoric ports in the south-western section of the harbour, to the Roman port, Saxon port, medieval and finally modern ports. In each case the new port was on a different location, frequently far away from its predecessor. In addition to all of this there is another layer of activity, as minerals have been extracted from the land around Poole Harbour for millennia. Purbeck stone and Purbeck marble were first quarried in Roman times, becoming a major trade during the medieval period. Clay took over in the seventeenth century, pottery works developed, and finally, in the twentieth century oil .

In 2004 a bronze axe was found by a diver just inside the mouth of Poole Harbour, nothing else was found around it and from its location it is almost certain that it had been lost from a boat, either fallen overboard or through the vessel sinking. The axe had been packed tight with another tool, a little gouge, of a type that is uncommon in England, but more widely found on the continent. Perhaps this axe is evidence of the earliest international traders to come to Poole.

The earliest evidence for any sort of port comes from Green Island, where imported pottery, mostly amphorae which probably originally contained wine, have been found.

Boy Scouts surveying the Green Island causeway in 1959.

Descriptions of the Iron Age and Romano-British site at Hamworthy by the schoolboys who excavated it in the 1920s.

Offshore islands or peninsulas were frequently used as early ports. Similar sites have been found at other places along the coast of Southern England. But what makes Green Island unique are the massive harbour installations.

In 1954 two stone structures were discovered, one running from Green Island towards the mainland, the other longer one from Cleavel Point on the mainland towards the island. They were first suspected to be the remains of a link between the island and the shore and were named the 'Green Island Causeway'. In 1959 an initial survey was carried out by a party of Boy Scouts. They did a remarkable job with minimal equipment and showed that the 'causeway' was an artificial structure, built of stone but with timber supports, discovered at the landward end, in the part now buried under intertidal mud. Unfortunately they found noting to date the structure. The causeway was then virtually forgotten for forty years, until 1999 when the Poole Harbour Heritage Project began work.

The project uncovered two stone structures. One was 160 metres long and between eight and ten metres wide running out from Cleavel Point on the mainland, the other 55 metres long projecting from Green Island, with a 70 metre gap between. Divers found nothing in this gap, which suggested that, rather than being a causeway, the stone structures are the remains of two harbour piers. Timbers recovered from the mainland pier have been radiocarbon dated to about 250 BC, making it the oldest constructed port in North West Europe.

Later in the Iron Age, about 50BC the settlement at Cleavel Point, on the Ower Peninsula, just across from Green Island seems to have been the main point of entry for imported goods. When the site was excavated in 1978 so much material connected with Brittany was found that the excavator suggested that families fleeing the Roman invasion of Gaul may have settled here as refugees.

When the Romans finally arrived in Poole Harbour, around AD 45, they don't seem to have come to Cleavel Point, rather they built a fort at Hamworthy. There had been a small Iron Age settlement there before and it appears that the fort was to protect a military depot. Supplies and equipment were landed here, taken up the new Roman road through Broadstone to the large military supply base at Lake Farm, which now lies below the Wimborne By-pass. Within a few years the fort had ceased to have any military function and the forts ditches were being used as a salt-works – swords into ploughshares.

The earliest investigation of the settlements on the Hamworthy Peninsula took place during the 1920s and '30s, under the guidance of the remarkable H. P. Smith. Harry Smith

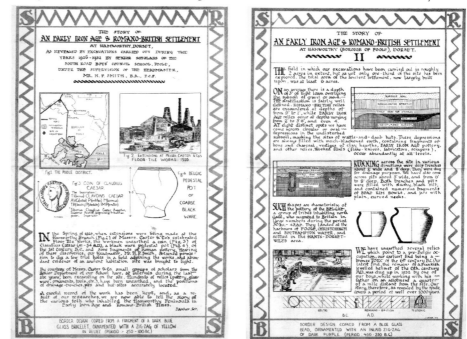

was a local school teacher who enthused his pupils with a love of their town's history, for decades archaeological finds were brought to 'Mr Smith', by his pupils and former pupils. So when the son of one of the staff at Pilkington's Glass Factory at Hamworthy brought Roman pottery to his teacher, H. P. Smith was in a

perfect position to organise a rescue excavation. His boys provided the labour whilst the artistic amongst them produced some amazing descriptive sheets. These were widely praised, duplicated and sent out to other schools to show what could be done. Smith never found the fort, (that wasn't discovered until the 1990s), but what he found was an Iron Age settlement that continued into the Roman period.

By late Roman times the settlements on Cleavel Point and Hamworthy seem to have declined, and no one knows if there was a major port in Poole Harbour from about the fourth century to the sixth. Then Wareham develops as the main port.

In the early seventh century there was a Christian church in Wareham, and several ancient memorial stones were found when the oldest part of the church was demolished in the early nineteenth century. By the eighth century Wareham was an international port. It was to Wareham that Aldhelm, then Abbot of Malmesbury, came on a journey to Rome. Here he had to wait for a suitable ship and whilst he was waiting he built a church somewhere nearby, perhaps at Corfe or Kingston.

As the Viking attacks became more serious Wareham was protected by King Alfred, massive walls were built surrounding the town. A century later the Vikings took the town, recognising its importance; around this time it appears on a map drawn by an Arab geographer. News of Wareham's existence had reached North Africa.

The Normans too realised how important Wareham was and built a castle, this was besieged and taken at least three different times during the civil wars between Stephen and Matilda. It is possible that it was this fighting that was to lead indirectly to the decline of Wareham, and the appearance of the port of Poole.

It has been suggested that the frequent fighting around Wareham in the years 1142 to 1144 may have led to some of the merchants there deciding to off load cargoes at a safe location at the top of the Wareham Channel, where the oyster fishermen had been coming for years. The first buildings of the new town at Poole were built on top of a massive layer of oyster shells.

Eighth century tombstone with the inscription CATGUG.C…[FI] LIUS GIDEO or Cadogan the son of Gideon.

Eighth century tombstone with the inscription DENIEL FI[LIUS …]AUPRIT IA[CET or Deniel the son of …auprit lies here.

The Saxon town walls of Wareham, built on the orders of Alfred the Great.

The castle mound at Wareham. It was the constant sieges of this castle during the civil war of Stephen and Matilda which may have led to local merchants creating the town of Poole for safety.

When Domesday Book was written in 1086 there was no Poole: the manors of Hamworthy and Canford (which included the future site of the town) are described but not Poole. The name is first recorded in about 1180, by 1224 it was an important enough port to be asked to supply ships to the King, and in the charter of about 1248 special mention is made of foreign merchants, allowing them to conduct legal business whenever they wanted rather than wait for the bi-monthly manorial courts. In little more than 100 years Poole had grown from virtually nothing into a port with international trade links.

John Hutchin's 1774 map of Wareham showing how the town had decreased in size, much of the land inside the walls being given over to fields and gardens.

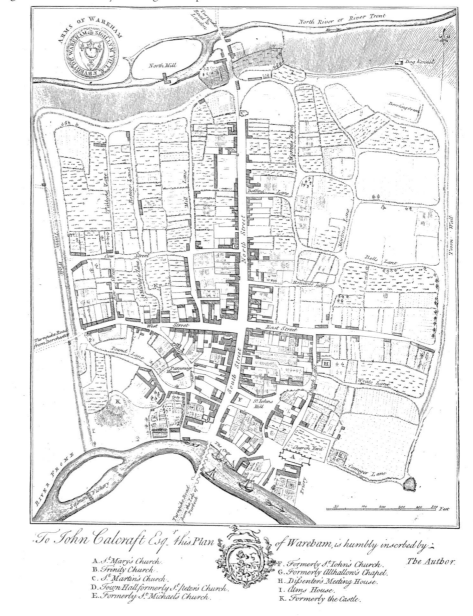

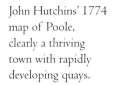

John Hutchins' 1774 map of Poole, clearly a thriving town with rapidly developing quays.

One of the main exports from Poole Harbour was Purbeck marble, this was usually shipped out through Ower Quay in the south western section of the harbour. This was also the landing place for supplies for Corfe Castle. Despite is importance it was little more than a landing place with one or two houses. Possibly spurred on by the amazing growth in Poole in 1286 Edward I commanded;

> Richard de Bosco and Walter de Marisco to lay out with sufficient streets and
> lanes and adequate sites for a market and church, and plots for merchants and
> others, a new town with a harbour in a place called *Gotower super mare*
> [Goathorn?], in the parish of Studland and on the King's land which was
> late of Robert Muchegros and contiguous to the said place, the lands and
> tenements of which the said Newtown the King is prepared to commit to
> merchants and others willing to take them, and to enfeoff them thereof for
> building and dwelling purposes.

Newton Bay, somewhere here the failed town of Newton was planned. Now there are just fields and a farm that has perpetuated the name.

For the past fifty years it has become a harmless sport amongst Dorset archaeologists to try and find the location of Newton. It is a certainly a pleasant way of spending a day or two as Newton Bay, lying to the north of Goathorn is a lovely place, but despite all this searching nothing definite has ever been found. It is quite possible that no town was ever even begun, plots may have been marked out with posts but no merchant ever came forward wishing to live there. The reason is easy to see. Poole has a deep water Channel running from the shore to the mouth of the harbour, whereas Newton Bay is shallow, the Ower Channel is narrow and difficult of access, the new town of *Gotower super mare* had little chance of succeeding.

If Newton was a failure Poole was an outstanding success, by the fourteenth century the list of imports and exports showed that Poole was exporting fish, salt and corn and importing iron, oil, coal and wine. Around the same time it seems to have had to call in outside help to settle a dispute with Wareham. Understandably Wareham had watched with fear the growth of its new rival, particularly one which any ship wanting to travel to Wareham would have to pass. There had clearly been tensions and in 1364 the Mayor of Winchelsea (one of the Cinque Ports in Sussex) presented Poole with a certificate giving details of the bounds of the Port.

Two trade bills from the early nineteenth century when coasting trade was very important in Poole. Much of this trade, particularly from the inland towns listed here was to disappear when the railways developed.

Though of no legal value whatsoever it was held in great respect in Poole, and was always read during the beating of the bounds of the port.

By the beginning of the fifteenth century Poole was an important town, with mayor and corporation, the main customs port for Dorset, but its rapid growth was still remembered. John Leland in the 1540s wrote:

> *Pole* is no Town of auncient occupying in Marchantdise : but rather of old Tyme a poore Fisshar Village and an Hammelet or Member to the Paroche Chirch. Ther be Men alyve that saw almost al the Town of *Pole* kyverid with Segge and Risshis.
>
> [*Poole* is no ancient merchant town: but rather of it was once a poor fishing village and hamlet without even a parish church. There are men alive that saw almost all the town of *Poole* covered with Sedges and Rushes.]

Baltic schooners in Poole just after the First World War, the last of the line of elegant sailing merchantmen that once dominated the local trade.

In 1568 Poole became a County Corporate, a separate county from Dorset, and around the same time its great trade began. Every year ships sailed from Poole to Newfoundland returning loaded with dried and salted fish, the Newfoundland merchants grew rich, their sons lived part of their lives in North America before returning to Poole. In Newfoundland there are houses, copies of ones first built in Dorset. The flat bottomed Poole canoe, designed for the shallow water of the harbour gave rise to traditional boat types in Canada. Whilst around the town there are still traces of this trade, the simplest, and perhaps the most evocative can be found in the Parish Church of St James. Rebuilt in 1821 the pillars are wooden, made from Newfoundland timber as sturdy as ships masts and apt for the church of what is now one of the great ports of Britain.

CHRISTCHURCH

Christchurch, like Poole has moved, but unlike Poole only one major move took place. In the late Iron Age, there was a major international port at Hengistbury Head. It was here, in excavations in 1911-12, that pre-Roman continental pottery were first recorded, showing that this was an international port. Unlike Poole there were no massive harbour installations,

The interior of St James' church Poole, the pillars are made from Newfoundland pine, usually brought into Poole for ships' masts.

Hengistbury Head,
the ancient
predecessor to
Christchurch. The
double Dykes, the
massive defensive
earthworks, can
clearly be seen
crossing the
headland.

rather an artificial 'hard' was created where boats were beached for loading and unloading. Where Hengistbury is remarkable is that this was an Iron Age mint, where coins of a distinctive shape were made. They were cast rather than stamped, and can be found throughout much of Dorset, the ancient territory of the Durotriges. Hengistbury Head is also remarkable as it is the probably the most visible prehistoric port in the country, with massive defensive ditches known as the Double Dykes.

There is only a little evidence of the Romans ever being in Hengistbury or Christchurch. It seems that the port had either been abandoned, or had seriously declined, when the Romans arrived. There is a story that a Roman shipwreck was once discovered in the harbour:

> In March last (1910) portions of a burnt and mud-buried Roman ship were discovered in the harbour near Christchurch. It was thought at first to be a Viking ship, but further excavations having since been made, it is now believed to be Roman. A small incense-cup or vase was found amongst the burnt timbers and sent to the British Museum for examination, with the result that Dr C. H. Read replied: "The small vase is of Roman date." Altogether, more than twenty articles – iron, bronze and pottery – have been recovered, with fragments of human remains. The small cup or vase is of bright red ware, and wheel turned. It was partly broken but most of the fragments are to hand, and can be restored. It is one of the smallest incense-cups found in England of Roman make, being 2 5/8 inches in diameter, and 3 ½ inches high, while the neck is 1 inch long. It is of very graceful outline and proportion. In the *Victoria County History* Christchurch is not considered to be a place of Roman occupation, and this is one of the first authentic finds made belonging to the Roman period, with the exception of a few coins. The site of the discovery is in private ground, and further results are expected.

Although described as a shipwreck, the description suggests something very different. First it was clearly found on land, the 'excavations' were on 'private grounds', then apart from the timbers the finds, small pottery vessels together with items of bronze and iron, and importantly human remains, would suggest a grave. This suggests that what was found was a remarkable well preserved timber lined grave. Fascinating, rare but not a ship.

Christchurch appears in the records in the early eighth century as Tweoxneam or Twyneham, or 'between two waters', a reference to the location of the new port at the junction of the Avon and Stour. It doesn't appear in any of the accounts of the Viking raids and seems to have been fairly unimportant until the eleventh century. There had been a small religious foundation here in Saxon times, however the Normans built a huge church and endowed it to create a great monastic establishment. This didn't affect the port which seems to have remained fairly small. There are few references to Christchurch as a medieval port, small cargoes of wine and wool are mentioned and on only one occasion was a ship from Christchurch requisitioned by the King for his navy (in 1303).

One unusual party of visitors were a group of French monks, who arrived with a terrible story but left a beautiful memorial in fine carving in the Priory:

> The Prior's doorway is said to owe its decorative carvings to some French monks who took refuge in Christchurch Haven some time in the thirteenth century, their vessel having been, they declared, chased out of its course by a terrible dragon. They were, it is further related, hospitably received by the then head of the Priory, with whom they dwelt for a considerable time, rewarding him for his goodness to them by aiding him in the care of the beautiful Sanctuary in which they were privileged to worship.

Dragons are generally scarce in this part of the country, though one was killed at Bisterne a few miles up the Avon around the same time:

> Sir Moris Barldey the sonne of Sir John Barkley, of Beverston, beinge a man of great strength and courage, in his tyme there was bread in Hampshire neere Bistherne a devouring Dragon, who doing much mischief upon men and cattell and could not be destroyed but spoiled many in attempting it, making his den neere unto a Beacon. This Sr Moris Barkley armed himself and encountered with it and at length overcam and killed it but died himself soone after.

When the Priory was dissolved in 1539 one of the mainstays of local trade went, the port declined even more, just dealing with a little local trade. But within a few years plans were afoot to turn Christchurch into a major port. In 1623 John Taylor, a London waterman (someone who was licensed to use a boat on the Thames) came to Christchurch. As well as a waterman he was a rather eccentric character, poet, traveller and promoter of various schemes. He was keen to promote water travel around and within Britain (he described coaches as the invention of the devil!). He sailed down the Thames and around the coast of south east England, describing it in verse, until:

> For having past, with perill, and much paine,
> And plow'd, and furrow'd o're the dangerous maine,
> O're depths, and flats, and many a ragged rock,
> We came to Christ-Church hav'n at five a clock.

He then turned to prose to propose to both describe his voyage up the Avon and to encourage the idea of making the Avon fully navigable as far as Salisbury.

> By which meanes of navigation, the whole city and countrey would be

relieved, loyterers turned into labourers, penurie into plenty and, to the glory
of God, the dignity and reputation of your citie, and the perpetuall worthy
memory of all benefactors, and well-willers unto so noble a worke.

The civil war intervened and nothing happened for fifty years, then in 1664 the River Avon
Navigation Act was passed giving permission for making the Avon navigable from
Christchurch to Salisbury. Work began in 1675 and by 1684 barges reached Salisbury. Then
severe floods damaged the works and, although the damage was repaired, they had cost so
much that the canal was never profitable and ceased operation by the 1730s.

At the same time there work started on improving Christchurch Harbour. The land had
been bought in 1665 by Edward, Earl of Clarendon. He had not long been Lord of the
Manor of Christchurch before it occurred to him that the estuary might be converted into
a harbour suitable for large vessels. He employed Andrew Yarranton a notable engineer of
the time who, in due course made his report.

About eighteen months since I was taken down by the Lord Clarendon to
Salisbury to survey the River of Avon to find whether the river might be
made navigable : As also whether a safe Harbour could be made at Christ-
Church for ships to come in and out and lye safe. After I had surveyed the
river I found it might with ease be made Navigable. I then with several others
went to sea several times, to sound and find the depths and to discover what
the Anchorage was. …. I waited upon the Lord Clarendon and some other
gentlemen to Sea, and there did discover to them the Reasons at large, having
convinc't them upon the place, of the fitness and conveniency in making a
Harbour there. At which time I observed two great things that place was
capable of. The First is At that very place where the Harbour may be made,
there may at any time safely come in and quietly ride at least 50 or 60 fifth
and sixth Rate Frigats; and that which is more strange, within three hundred
yards of the place there is a Hill or Promontory, which was an old Camp of
the Romans or Saxons as it is said, which will lodge a hundred thousand men
and in three days may be made so defensible, that no Army (be it never so
great) will be able to annoy them, all parts of the said Camp being defended
by Sea except about three hundred yards, and that is intrenched by a very
deep Ditch, yet very useful, and Relief by Sea may be brought to this place
every Tide, and no Party by Land, as it now is, can give any opposition.

Work begun, a new entrance was cut across Mudeford Spit and a massive pier built. Then
the money ran out, Lord Clarendon was impeached for treason and had to flee the county,
storms damaged what had been begun. The work stopped, the entrance to the harbour
reverted to its natural form and nothing was left, apart from fragments of the pier, now
called the Clarendon Rocks, and up the Avon valley the remains of the old canal, primitive
locks at Downton and Britford and long straight sections of the river close to Salisbury.

As with Bridport, the idea of improving the harbour didn't go away. One spectacular
failure didn't stop other people dreaming. The great engineer John Smeaton, the designer
of the third, and successful, Eddystone Lighthouse, came in 1762. He said that it could
never be a major port, but he thought it could be improved. He made his plans, but the
proposers of the plan dropped it as they couldn't raise the money. Other proposals followed,
in 1836 and again in the 1860s, but nothing happened. The only real attempts to improve
the harbour were carried out by the organisation which almost destroyed it, the Hengistbury
Head Mining Company. The story of the environmental disaster it caused is told in another

The approach to
Town Quay, a
complex entrance
only suitable for
small vessels, which
led to the decline of
Christchurch as a
port.

chapter. In the late 1840s the company was bringing coal in on barges towed by a steam ship. In order to make loading of the ironstone easier a short canal was cut through the saltmarshes on the northern side of Hengistbury Head and a dock was built at its end. This worked very well, as long as there was readily available ironstone and the company was profitable. As soon as the ironstone became difficult to mine, the company sold up and the dock was abandoned. It is still there, now a feeding pace for wading birds.

Other trade coming to Christchurch was very light. It mostly consisted of coastal trade, ships calling in on the way to somewhere else to drop off part of their cargo. In 1803 there was little more than one ship a week arriving or leaving, and this should have been a high point of coastal trade. When the railway reached Christchurch in 1862 most of this trade vanished. The little that did survive wasn't helped by the attitude of some of the skippers. The son of the owner of one of the last trading vessels of Christchurch Harbour recalled:

'Charlotte' would arrive in the bay and stand off. After a few days Dad would take me in his pony and trap to Mudeford and go out to her. One of the fishermen would row us out in a pot boat. Dad would hammer on the side and from below this bearded head would appear. 'When are you taking her in?'. The master would say 'When wind and tide suit', always the same answer. 'But you've been here a week', 'When wind and tide suit'. Dad would never go on board, He'd inherited the ship and another one but never went aboard.

When wind and tide did suit Dick Selwood would sail her a little into the harbour. She had a boy on board – the rest of the crew. They had a big dingy, about fourteen or fifteen foot. The boy would skull the dingy ahead with the anchor in it and then drop the anchor. Dick would wind on the winch and bring the barge up to her anchor. They'd put it back in the dingy and skull it out again. The 'Charlotte' was so heavily laden that she didn't drift much with her sails down. There were no engines in those days. That's how they got her up to the Quay where she was unloaded by baskets.

The description of how the sailing barge was dragged up to the Quay gives a clear idea as to why skippers didn't like calling at Christchurch. By the First World War Christchurch had ceased as a working port. From then on it was used by a few small fishermen and, increasingly, pleasure craft.

PIRACY

Piracy is essentially theft at sea. Whilst popular stories and films have jolly pirates in sunny sea, usually the West Indies, piracy was a serious problem along the British coast in the past. As well as individual pirates, ports would deliberately attack one another's ships, in 1265 the king ordered an inquiry into the mutual injuries inflicted upon each other at sea by the men of Lyme and Dartmouth, which had led to 'enormous transgressions and homicides' by both parties. Sixty years later:

> 1322. May 20. York. The like [commission of oyer and terminer] to Robert de Stokheye, John de Treiagu, and John de Fosse, on complaint by William de Ebbeworth of Tavystok, by petition exhibited before the king and council, that, whereas he lately freighted a ship called the *Edmund of Plemmewe* [Plymouth] with cloth, linen, canvas, iron, wax, and other goods for conveyance to Sutton, certain persons of the towns of Waymewe [Weymouth] and Portland and the neighbouring parts attacked the ship on her voyage to Sutton during one whole day and more, and at last boarded her in the port of the water of Lyme on the confines of the counties of Devon and Dorset, carried away the said merchandise, scuttled the ship and sunk her in the said port, and assaulted the mariners, merchants and others that were in her; the jury to be of the said counties.

Whilst the crown could deal fairly easily when towns fell out, individual pirates were more difficult, especially during periods such as the French wars. For example in 1402 the famous Henry Pay, of Poole, was charged with piracy, whilst only two years later he was hired to raise a number of ships for the king.

In 1429 Studland is first mentioned as the favoured pirate base, when the crews of the *James* of Studland and *Welfare* of Swanage, drove ashore a foreign ship and then plundered her.

Dorset became a haven for pirates in the early years of Queen Elizabeth's reign. Ports such as Weymouth would give them shelter, and there were plenty of merchants willing to buy stolen goods from them. In one case, a juryman, at a trial of a suspected pirate, confessed himself a dealer with pirates! Another pirate claimed that he had contacts with twenty one dealers in Weymouth, Melcombe, and the nearby villages.

The 1580s marked the high point (or low point depending on your point of view) of Dorset's involvement with piracy. In 1580 a two pirates, Clinton Atkinson and Philip Boyte of Portland captured an Italian ship carrying a cargo from the West Indies worth £1300. They sold it at Weymouth and Topsham in Devon, but were soon caught, Philip Boyte was sent to London and hung, Clinton Atkinson was held for trial in Exeter but bribed the jailor and escaped. The same year the *Sea Horse* and *Master of the Sea* from the Baltic were brought into Studland, which was now the pirates' chief base, where their cargoes were sold. In the following year the pirate Stephen Heynes is first mentioned. He was a particularly evil man who would torture his captives if he though there was money hidden on board,

Lulworth Cove, in the 1560s the haunt of pirates.

Studland Bay, the hell on earth where pirates gathered, and where they were finally hunted down.

'so that some have lost their thumbs and fingers and others their sight and hearing'. The list of ships taken into Studland Bay and their cargoes sold is a long one, the *Grace of God*, the *Marie*, the *Esperance* (French), *Our Lady of Conception* (Spanish), the *Anne* of Plymouth and the *Hirundine* (English) and many more. At this time Studland was a wild place, of one of the innkeepers there it was said, 'William Mundaye of Studland, his howse is the hell of the worlde and he the divell'. When a captured ship arrived local men would come to Studland in the hope of a bargain. A bribe would be sent to the Vice Admiral of Dorset in Corfe Castle and then the 'fair' would begin. The local gentry would arrive to make merry with the pirates. Notable amongst them was Henry Howard, son of Viscount Bindon; when word of his behaviour reached his father in London, he had him sent to prison for a while!

All seemed to be going well for the pirates, the authorities in London seemed powerless and local officials could easily be threatened or bribed. Then they began to overreach themselves, thinking that no one could touch them. Captain John Piers, a Cornishman, began the decline by capturing a local vessel, the *Anne* of Lulworth sailing from Cherbourg to Weymouth, bringing the vessel into Studland Bay for sale. Captain Piers was promptly arrested. He thought bribing the jailor in Dorchester was all he needed to escape, but he reckoned without Henry Howard, who had disliked his time in prison and had no wish to return. Howard recaptured Piers, made sure he was held securely in Corfe Castle and oversaw the trial. Piers was hung at Studland, 'to the terryfying of others for that same place hathe bene muche frequented and the inhabitantes molested with pirats'.

Thomas Walton (alias Purser) then made another blunder, he made a, 'very insolent and rebellious attempt', attacking several French and English ships in Weymouth Road. He captured one French ship, then a group of Weymouth men sailed out to counter attack, the pirates were driven off losing seven men. Angered by this Walton demanded compensation, the town refused and instead purchased ordnance and munitions. Rather than fight, Walton returned to Studland, where the situation was about to change.

Francis Hawley, Vice Admiral of Purbeck, had long complained that he could do nothing about the pirates since, 'they are so strong and well-appointed as they cannot be on the sudden repulsed' and asked for munitions. Then in June 1583 help came, the government appointed William Aboroughe, clerk to the Navy and Benjamin Gunson, gentleman to the commands of the *Bark Talbot* and *Unica* respectively. These two unlikely heroes fell upon the pirates like a pair of sea eagles and within a few weeks had rounded most of them up. Thomas Walton was captured after a fight in mid channel with the *Bark Talbot* as was Clinton Atkinson. The *Unica* chased another ship onto the shore near Boscombe, the captain William Valentine tried to hide in a nearby inn, but was captured.

The gallows on Baiter Point, Poole, the final destination for many of the violent pirates and smugglers who infested the coast.

The pirates were taken to London, questioned then condemned and tried (in that order, the list identifying who was to hang was written before their trial!). Clinton Atkinson and Thomas Walton were hung at Wapping. One pirate received a pardon, and immediately reneged on it. He was William Arnewood, who returned to his old ways. However the town of Weymouth was now totally opposed to the pirates and fitted out two ships, the *Archangel* and the *Salomon* to hunt him down. They caught him in Lulworth Cove, and with the imprisonment of John Uvedale the Mayor of Corfe, who had been the principal receiver of the stolen goods, peace returned to Studland.

SMUGGLING

About a hundred and fifty years ago, just after smuggling ceased to be a serious problem, people began to regard smugglers as genial rogues, pitting their wits against the wicked Revenue men. Then they were seen as champions of the common people opposed to a corrupt government, who had imposed massive and unjust taxes on the poor. They have been compared very favourably with modern drug smugglers and their behaviour has been held up in contrast to the violence and intimidation which accompanies the modern 'trade'.

Nothing could be farther from the truth. Eighteenth century governments might have been corrupt, but they weren't stupid. There was no point in taxing the poor, they hadn't got any money, it made much more sense to tax the rich, in particular tax the luxuries which were not vital for everyday life but for which the rich were prepared to pay a considerable amount. Smuggling soon made considerable economic sense. Cargoes would be purchased in France or the Channel Islands and brought to a pre-arranged spot on the coast where they would be unloaded and carried inland for distribution.

> Persons engaged in smuggling-ventures used to go round the country like mercantile travellers, and ask gentlemen what they would "give to have a pipe or hogshead of wine put into their cellar." The price being agreed on, it was only a question of conveyance.

To stop them were only a few Revenue men, the 'Riding Officers', and if they caught a smuggler it was often very different to get a conviction. Smugglers, generally, had a reputation for violence. Anyone who crossed a smuggler might be beaten up or killed, as a lesser 'punishment' men were taken to France and abandoned there. To be dumped in a

The raid on the Poole Customs House.

foreign country, with which England was quite likely at war, with no money and knowledge of the language, was frequently a prolonged death sentence. Very few men who were so abandoned ever returned home. People whose death or disappearance might provoke too many questions were usually bribed.

From all along the Dorset coast come tales of violence and murder. The raid on the Poole Customs House gives some idea of the organisation that some group of smugglers could achieve.

In September, 1747, one John Diamond, or Dymar, agreed with a number of smugglers, to go over to the island of Guernsey, to smuggle tea, where, having purchased a considerable quantity, on their return in a cutter, they were taken by one captain William Johnson, who carried the vessel and tea to the port of Poole, and lodged the tea in the custom-house there.

The smugglers being very much incensed at this miscarriage of their purchase, resolved not to sit down contented with the loss; but, on a consultation held among them, they agreed to go and take away the tea from the warehouse where it was lodged. Accordingly, a body of men, to the number of sixty, well armed, assembled in Charlton forest, and from thence proceeded on their enterprise; to accomplish which they agreed, that only thirty of them should go upon the attack, and that the remaining thirty should be placed as scouts upon the different roads, to watch the motions of the officers and soldiers, and to be ready to assist or alarm the main body, in case any opposition should be made.

The party deputed for the purpose arrived at Poole, about eleven o'clock on the night of the 6th of October, 1747; when having ridden down a little back lane, they came to the sea-side; they here quitted their horses, leaving two of the gang to look after them, whilst the remainder proceeded to the custom-house, which they broke into with violence, and having broken open four doors, reached the warehouse in which the tea had been deposited. This, which amounted to about two tons weight, they secured and carried off. They carefully abstained from touching any other property, swearing that they came for their own, and would have it.

They returned with their booty through Fordingbridge, in Hampshire, where some hundreds of people were assembled to view the cavalcade. Among the spectators was Daniel Chater, a shoemaker, known to Diamond, who shook hands with him as he passed along, and threw him a bag of tea.

His Majesty's proclamation coming out, with a promise of a reward for apprehending those persons who were concerned in breaking open the custom-house; and Diamond having been taken into custody at Chichester, on suspicion of having been one of them : Chater mentioned the meeting at Fordingbridge, which coming to the knowledge of the collector of the customs at Southampton, he sent William Galley (a king's officer) with Chater, to convey a letter to major Battin, a justice of the peace for Sussex, the purport of which was to desire an examination of Chater, in relation to what he knew of the affair, and whether he could prove the identity of Diamond's person.

These two unfortunate men were entrapped by a gang of smugglers, who had obtained information of their journey. A maidservant in an alehouse realised who they were and gave them strong drink to make them sleepy then sent a messenger to the gang. The two men were woken by being whipped, tied to a horse, and whipped until both were nearly dead. The gang first killed the customs officer Galley by burying him alive. They kept Chater chained up in a shed for a few more days then he was attacked with a knife, thrown head first down a thirty foot well, and large stones thrown down on him until he was dead.

The crime was brought to light six or seven months afterwards, by the confession of one of the murderers whilst in custody on some other charge. Fifteen smugglers were concerned in the murder, many of whom were apprehended, and a special commission was issued to try them at Chichester, the crime having been committed in the county of Sussex. The trials lasted from the 16th to the 19th April, 1748. Seven of the prisoners were convicted and executed. On the 4th April, in the same year, five of the smugglers concerned in breaking open the custom-house at Poole, were indicted at the Old Bailey for that offence, and for stealing from the said custom-house, thirty-seven hundred-weight of tea, value 500 and upwards, on Oct. 6, 1747. Four of them were convicted, of whom one was afterwards pardoned, and three others being executed.

On other occasions the smugglers were even prepared to take on the Royal Navy.

To: Custom House, London
From: Custom House, Cowes
20th July 1784

Hon. Sirs

On the 16th Inst. Two large Lugsail vessels were brought into this Port by the Officers of the 'Orestes' Sloop of War having been seized in Christchurch harbour by them in conjunction with Mr James Sarmon Commander of an Excise Revenue Cutter and Mr George Sarmon Commander of the 'Swan' Cutter in the service of this Port for having the proceeding day unlawfully imported and run a large quantity of tea and foreign spirits near Christchurch Head within the limits of the Port of Southampton.

We are sorry to acquaint your Honours that the Officers were oppos'd, obstructed and wantonly fired upon when rowing into Christchurch Harbour and before they had landed or taken possession of the vessels by a number of smugglers assembled on board the Lugger and on the shore. Mr Allen, master of the 'Orestes' was shot and is since dead and one of the mariners wounded in the arm. An inquest has been taken on the body of Mr Allen. The Jury having returned a verdict of Wilful Murder. The Coroner has issued warrants for the arrest of William Parrott and William May, two persons suspected to have been accessories in the Murder; none of the rest are yet known or discovered. A transaction of this kind having happened in the face of day, and so near Christchurch it is more than probable that many of the persons assembled on the spot must be known in that neighbourhood especially as the smugglers sheltered in a Public House called the Haven House from the windows of which, and the stable adjoining, several muskets were fired at the Officers.

We have judged it necessary to write to Mr Jeanes, supervisor of the riding Officers at Christchurch, to excite him to use his endeavours to apprehend the offenders and to transmit any information he may collect that is likely to lead to a discovery of any persons concerned in the Murder.

Never was a more unprovoked attach made on Officers of the Revenue than in the present instance and it shows how necessary exemplary punishment is for such daring violators of the law.

The smugglers had not even the pretence to urge of firing in their own defence, for many shots were fire on the Officers from behind sand banks and sheltered places and Mr Allen who was first wounded in the thigh and afterwards in the body received his death would before a single gun was fired by the Revenue Officers.

The smugglers also had another card up their sleeve: Mr Jeanes, head of the Customs at Christchurch was in their pay. Two years later he was caught, and even then all that could be done was dismiss him.

Order to dismiss J S Jeans as supervisor of Riding Officers from Board of Customs in London May 1786

In July 1784 when the 'Orestes' sloop of war attempted to seize two large smuggling Luggers commanded by May and Parrott in Christchurch Harbour, when the said Jeans positively ordered the Riding Officers not to take any notice or make any remark in their Journal, of the transactions of the day although the Master of the 'Orestes' was murdered by the smugglers in the execution of his duty.

We deem the said Jeans unworthy of any further trust in the service of the Revenue and have therefore dismissed him therefore.

Eventually one of the smugglers was convicted of the crime.

Winchester Saturday Jan 28 1786

George Coombes, who in the June sessions was convicted of aiding and abetting in the murder of W Allen, late master of the sloop Orestes, in the harbour of Christchurch, who on information of there being smuggled goods on shore, manned his boat in order to proceed on shore, but the boat striking

Looking across Stanpit Marshes to Christchurch, the site of the battle of Christchurch between local smugglers and the Royal Navy.

on the sand, he got in the water to set her afloat, when a ball from a gun on shore shot him of which he died; the verdict was left for the opinion of the Judges, which being delivered by Mr Justice Willes, the prisoner received sentence to be executed on Tuesday morning at Execution Dock.

He went out of Newgate at a quarter past 12 O'clock, attended by the proper Admiralty Officers, and the silver oar carried before him. He behaved with that decency which became his untimely end.

The body of the above unfortunate young fellow is ordered by the Court of Admiralty to be hung in chains near Christchurch Harbour, where the fact was committed.

On other occasions the smugglers' crimes went unpunished. The Rev. Richard Warner, writing in 1830 recalled his schooldays at Christchurch where:

The father of one of my school-fellows, a Mr Bursey, who was for some years one of the Christchurch Custom House officials, and lived at the village of Milton, was aroused from sleep one dark winter night by a loud rapping on the door.

On looking through the casement window he perceived two men though their countenances were not distinguishable through the gloom of midnight. He enquired their business; when one of them informed him that he had discovered a large quantity of smuggled goods in a contiguous barn to which he and his companions would lead him if he would reward them with a stipulated sum. A bargain was immediately struck, the unsuspicious officer hastily clothed himself, descended unarmed into the passage, opened the door, and in one minute his brains were dashed out upon his own threshold.

The killers were never caught. Indeed many of the smugglers seem to have considered that they were in the right and the authorities in the wrong. If one of them died in a fight with the Revenue, he was clearly murdered. A gravestone in Kinson churchyard records:

To the memory of Robert Trotman late of Rond (Rowde) in the county of Wilts who was barbarously murdered on the shore near Poole the 24th March 1765.
A little tea one leaf I did not steal
For guiltless blood shed I to God appeal
Put tea in one scale human blood in t`other
And think what tis to slay a harmless brother

Whilst if you read the contemporary newspaper reports, it hardly sounds like cold blooded murder.

1765 Sherborne, March 30. Last Sunday Night a scuffle happened at the Sand Banks near Poole betwixt about 30 Smugglers who were conveying a large Quantity of Tea just landed and about one Half that Number of the Crew of a Cutter, stationed there to watch their Motions; in which one of the Smugglers, whose Name was Trotman, was killed on the spot, and there is Reason to believe several of them were wounded. Nine of their Horses were killed and about Twenty Hundred Weight of Tea taken. On the Side of the Cutter one Man was shot through the leg a Midshipman wounded in his head and otherwise much bruised. The Purser was beat in such a Manner, as to be left for dead, and was thrown within the Surf of the Sea, to be carried off by it, but luckily he recovered; he had also a Pistol discharged at his Breast, which luckily striking a Button, did no other Harm than bruising the Part below.

In Weymouth another gravestone tells of another crime and this time there can be no doubt it was murder.

> Sacred to the memory of Lieut. Thos Edward Knight, RN, of Folkestone, Kent, Aged 42, who in the execution of his duty as Chief Officer of the Coastguard was wantonly attacked by a body of smugglers near Lulworth on the night of 28th of June 1832, by whom after being unmercifully beaten he was thrown over the cliff near Durdle Door from the effects of which he died the following day.

The trade remained profitable until the end of the Napoleonic Wars, then two things happened. The first was the reorganisation of the coastguard. Now large numbers of men were employed along the coast, primarily concerned with the safe passage of vessels, but also with the prevention of smuggling. As they were predominantly manned by former Royal Navy men they were efficient and were helped by a government keen to prosecute any attempt at evading the Revenue. Then, as the nineteenth century progressed, the duties on many of the items smuggled began to drop. Falling profits and rising prosecutions swiftly led to the end of the old, large-scale smuggling.

WRECKING

The other illegal activity much practiced in the past along the Dorset coast and, indeed still practiced when the opportunity arises, is wrecking. This is not, and indeed never has been, the deliberate luring of ships onto the shore. Although there are stories that this once took place there are no contemporary court cases, complaints or any other documentary evidence for this practice. Instead wrecking is defined as the taking of objects from a shipwreck without the consent of its owner. People still seem to believe that it is permissible to take objects from a shipwreck, though they would never dream of taking things from a crashed car, though legally this is much the same.

Confusion began a long time ago over the ownership of unclaimed wreck, who owned the remains of a ship and cargo for which there was no apparent owner. By the middle ages this right had been vested in the crown, though the monarch could, and often did, grant this right to coastal landowners. Indeed many coastal landowners still have the rights to wreck today, the National Trust, for example, owns the right of wreck for much of the shoreline of the Isle of Purbeck.

These rights were frequently very badly defined leading to arguments as to who actually owned the rights to a particular shipwreck. Some local landowners claimed a right that wasn't theirs, and other people just saw a wreck as a source of profit. Despite many complaints, the looting of shipwrecks was commonplace around the coast for centuries. The children in the villages at the back of Chesil Beach would chant a macabre rhyme.

> Blow wind, Rise Storm,
> Bring us a ship on shore before morn!

It is a sad fact that, most of our records of early shipwrecks comes from the court cases concerning the looting of the ships:

Fifteenth-century gold coin found on the beach at Abbotsbury, evidence, perhaps, of a medieval shipwreck.

1305 A Spanish ship was driven by tempest on the coast near Portland, where the worn out mariners transferred themselves to the shore. Henry Blake and 260 others broke the ship, cut it to pieces and carried away the goods.

1306 A Bordeaux [ship] was lost under Corfe, and although some of the crew and two dogs escaped alive the people thereabouts carried away the cargo and destroyed the ship.

1311 Fernaldus Martyn and Peter de Garsi had said that when they were wrecked in the *St Goymelote*, on the sea coast near Abbotsbury the people there broke open their chests, when washed ashore, and appropriated 100 marks of gros Tournois (coins) & 100 marks sterling, together with other goods.

In 1747 a gold coin of Edward III (1325–62) was foind on the beach at Abbotsbury. It is tempting to associate such a loss with a shipwreck such as the last one.

Golden Grape, wrecked on Chesil Beach 1641
'On 11th. December last by extremity of fowle weather the shipp was forced on shore upon the beech in the Weste bay of Portland Island where she was broken to pieces, seven men and boyes drowned and the greatest part of the goods, moneys, plate and loading lost save onely such as were salved by some of the company of the said shipp, and by other people of the countrey who by force and violence tooke and carryed the same away.'

One of the most famous wrecks on the Dorset coast took place in 1749 with the loss of the Dutch vessel *De Hoop*, often anglicised as the *Hope*.

She was believed to be carrying more than £30000 in gold and other valuables, the results of successful trading in South America and on the Spanish Main. The ship ran onto the Chesil in the early hours of 16 January 1749. It was very dark and with no light from Portland lighthouses, either by reason of the great mist, or the neglect of the persons there. The *De Hoop* struck with great force and broke up very quickly, her crew were fortunately able to scramble to safety across a bridge formed by a broken mast. Within a few hours a mob from Portland and Weymouth were on the scene, followed by men from all over Dorset. and the neighbouring counties as news of the wreck spread. For ten days the beach was the site of frenzied digging as the shingle was turned over and over in the search for gold. It was later estimated that some ten thousand people had been on Chesil Beach. Fighting soon broke out continually, but it took armed soldiers to eventually dispersed the mob. The authorities acted rapidly to recover the looted treasure, much was recovered and a number of local men were brought before the magistrates. During the following summer assizes, Augustin Elliott, a labourer of Portland, appeared in the dock at Dorchester charged with "feloniously stealing and carrying away 10 oz. of gold and 20 oz of silver from the ship *Hope*, the property of Hentrick Hogenberg, a merchant of Amsterdam." The evidence was very strong and no one reading the reports of the court case today can doubt that Augustin Elliott was guilty. After a trial of six hours, to the surprise of many of the people there Elliott was found not guilty. It was later pointed out that with so many people having been involved in the looting it would be difficult to empanel a jury in Dorset that year, and not include

'Serious advice and Fair Warning', a sermon preached in 1754 on the evils of looting from shipwrecks. A more recent rector of Chickerell, where the sermon was originally preached, once tried it out to an empty church. It took nearly two and a half hours to preach.

SERIOUS ADVICE
AND
FAIR WARNING
To all that live upon the Sea-Coast of *England* and *Wales*,

PARTICULARLY

To thofe in the Neighbourhood of *Wey-mouth* and *Portland*;

Addreffed to them in a

SERMON

Preached the 22d of *December*, 1754, in the Churches of *Fleet* and *Chickerill*, on Occafion of feveral Shipwrecks at that Time upon the Coaft of *England*.

To which are added,

Some Extracts from the feveral Acts of Parliament relating to Ships that are ftranded on the Coaft, and the Penalties to be inflicted on all thofe that plunder the Merchants Goods.

By THOMAS FRANCKLYN, Rector of *Langton-Herring*, and Vicar of *Fleet* in the County of *Dorfet*,

LONDON:
Printed for A. LINDE, in *Catherine Street* in the *Strand*. M.DCC.LVI.

The wreck of the
Catherine, Mrs Burns
on the deserted ship.

someone who had been on the beach looking for gold! Over the years many people have
gone looking for the *De Hoop*, without success. In fact the wreck was smashed to pieces, most
of the treasure on board was recovered at the time, and whatever remains of the ship is
probably buried in the shingle of Chesil Beach.

In 1785 One of the worst disasters every to take place along the Dorset coast took
place when several ships of a fleet carrying a regiment to the West Indies were wrecked.
There is a remarkable, and dreadful, first hand account of the wreck from Mrs Burns, the
young wife of one of the junior officers. She was one of only two survivors from the ship
Catherine (her husband did not survive).

> The evening of the Seventeenth was boisterous and threatening; the Master
> said he was afraid we should have some bad weather, and indeed it proved to
> very tempestuous, that no rest was to be obtained. It was about ten o'clock
> in the morning of the Eighteenth when the Mate looked down into the cabin,
> and cried – "Save yourselves, if you can."
>
> The consternation and terror of that moment cannot be described I had
> a loose gown on, and wrapping it round me, I went up, not quite on the deck,
> but to the top of the stairs, from whence I saw the sea break mountains high
> against the shore, while the passengers and soldiers seemed thunderstruck by
> the sense of immediate and inevitable danger; and the seamen, too conscious
> of the hopelessness of any exertion, stood in speechless agony, certain that
> in a few minutes they must meet the destruction which menaced them.
>
> Suddenly a tremendous wave broke over the ship, and struck me with
> such violence, that I was for a moment stunned and, before I could recover
> myself, the ship struck with a force so great as to throw me from the stairs
> into the cabin. At the same moment the cabin, with a dreadful crash, broke
> in upon me and beams and planks threatened to bury me in ruins.
>
> A sense of my condition lent me strength to disengage myself from the
> boards and fragments that surrounded me, and I once more got up the stairs
> I hardly know how; but what a scene did I behold! The masts were all lying
> across the shattered remains of the deck, and no living creature appeared on
> it - all were gone! I looked forward to the shore; but there I could see nothing
> except the dreadful surf that broke against it, while behind the ship immense
> black waves rose like tremendous ruins; I knew that they must overwhelm it,
> and thought that there could be no escape for me.
>
> I sat almost inclosed by pieces of the wreck, and the water now reached

Objects from a late
eighteenth century
shipwreck off Fleet,
possibly the *Catherine*.

my breast. The bruises I had received made every exertion extremely difficult, and my loose gown was so entangled among the beams and pieces of the ship, that I could not disengage it. Still the desire of life, the hope of being welcomed on shore, whither I thought my friends had escaped, and the remembrance of my child, all united to give me courage to attempt saving myself. I therefore determined to make one effort to preserve my life; I disengaged my arms from my gown, and finding myself able to move, I quitted the wreck, and felt myself on the ground; I attempted to run, but was too feeble to save myself from a raging wave that overtook and overwhelmed me: then I believed myself gone, yet, half-suffocated as I was, I struggled very much, and I remember I thought I was very long dying! The wave left me - I breathed again, and made another attempt to get higher upon the bank; but then, quite exhausted, I fell down, and my senses forsook me!

By this time some of the people on the bank saw me, and two men came to my assistance. They lifted me up; I once more recovered some faint recollection as they bore me along, one of them said the sea would overtake us; that he must let me go, and take care of his own life. I only remember clinging to the other, and imploring him not to leave me to the merciless waves. But I have a very confused idea of what passed, till I saw the boat which I was to be put into, to cross the Fleet water. I had then only strength to say "For God's sake do not take me to sea again."

I believe the apprehension of it, added to my other sufferings, helped to deprive me of all further sensibility, for I have not the least recollection of any thing afterwards, till I was roused by the remedies applied to restore me in the farm-house, whither I was carried, and heard round me a number of women, who asked me a great many questions, which I was unable to answer. I remember hearing one say I was a French woman - another that I was a Negro and I was so bruised, and in such a disfigured condition, that the conjectures of these people were not surprising.

When I recovered some degree of confused recollection, and was able to speak, I begged they would let me go to a bed. I did not ask this, however, with any expectation of life, for I was now in such a state of suffering that my only wish was to be allowed to lie down in peace and die. Nothing could exceed the humanity of Mr. Abbot, the inhabitant of Fleet Farm House, nor the compassionate attention of his sister, Miss Abbot, who not only afforded me immediate assistance, but continued for some days after I got to Weymouth to attend me with such kindness and humanity as I shall always remember with the sincerest gratitude.

One of the survivors of the *Venus* had even less luck in getting help from the local people, who had descended on the beach in the hope of plunder.

Mr. Darley escaped by throwing himself from the wreck, at a moment when she drifted high on the stones: he reached them without broken limbs, but the furious sea overtook him, and carried him back, not, however, so far but that he regained the ground; and notwithstanding the weight of his clothes, and his exhausted state, he reached the top of the bank, but there the power of farther exertion failed him, and he fell. While he lay in this situation, trying to recover breath and strength a great many people from the neighbouring villages passed him - they had crossed the Fleet water in the hopes of sharing what the lower inhabitants of this coast are too much accustomed to consider as their right, the plunder of the ships wrecked on their shore and, in the gratification of their avarice, they are too apt to forget humanity. Scenes like these call forth the most honourable, and discover the most degrading qualities of the human heart.

Mr. Darley seems to have been so far from meeting with immediate assistance among here who were plundering the dead, without thinking of the living, (otherwise than to make some advantage of them also) that though he saw many boats passing and repassing the Fleet water, he found great difficulty in procuring a passage over for himself and two or three of his fellow sufferers, who had by this time joined him: having, however, at length passed it, he soon met with Mr Bryer, Surgeon of Weymouth, to whose active humanity all the unhappy sufferers were greatly indebted; on his reaching Weymouth, the gentlemen of the *South Gloucester* sent him every supply of necessaries that his situation required - and all the soldiers and sailors were taken care of by Mr. Warne, Agent to the Commissioners for the Sick and Hurt'

The following day Chesil Beach was a scene of horror:

The gentlemen leaving their horses at the Fleet farm-house, crossed the Fleet water, to the beach, and there, whatever idea had been formed of the scene they were now to witness, infinitely exceeded in horror by the spectacle before them. No celebrated field of carnage, where the heroes among mankind have gathered their bloodiest laurels, ever presented, in proportion to its size, a more fearful sight than the Chissel-bank now exhibited. It was strewn for two miles with the dead bodies of men and animals, with pieces of wreck and piles of plundered goods, which groups of people were at work to carry away, regardless of the sight of the drowned bodies that filled the newly-

A real 'souvenir of a shipwreck', a model of the *Napoli* made from wood recovered from the wreck.

arrived spectators with grief and amazement.

On the poor remains of these unfortunate victims death appeared in all its hideous forms and indeed the particulars cannot be given either the sea or the people who had first gone down to the shore, had stripped of every article of clothes, those who had probably ventured, or had been thrown by the shocks into the water with their clothes on, as some of the officers certainly were clothed at the fatal moment. The remains of a military stock or the wristbands and collars of the shirt, or a piece of blue pantaloons, were all of their clothes that were left: and when the rites of sepulchre were to be performed, the Lieutenant of the *South Gloucester*, who superintended the performance of this melancholy duty, had no other means of distinguishing some of the officers than by the different appearance of their hands from those of men who had been accustomed to hard labour.

The remains of that gallant officer, Captain Barcroft was known by the honourable scars that witnessed the wounds he had received in the service of his country. His mourning friends have, from that circumstance, the sad satisfaction of knowing that his body was rescued from the sea, and buried with military honours.

A hundred years later, in 1872, the situation hadn't improved when the *Royal Adelaide* was wrecked in Chesil Cove. At first all went as well as could be expected. The coastguard managed to get the rocket apparatus set up and sent a line out to the wreck. The vast majority of the passengers and crew were rescued, only seven were lost as the ship broke up before they could be brought safely to shore. Sadly this included an eight-year-old girl.

Some of the crowd that had gathered on the shore were helping the coastguard officers with the rescued passengers, the rest were waiting to see what they could get from the wreck. As she ship broke up casks of spirits drifted ashore. These were immediately broached by the waiting mob.

Drunkenness, Debauchery and Death!

was the headline in the local paper after the event. It was not an exaggeration. The night was a freezing one in late November and five people, including a teenaged boy, died of a mixture of alcohol and hypothermia, collapsing drunkenly on the beach where their bodies were found the next day. The crowds didn't stay long, they were swiftly driven away by the police and coastguard. This time some of the looters were caught. One man found with a large number of tools from the Royal Adelaide in his shed claimed that he had taken them as a 'souvenir', of the wreck. The magistrate didn't believe him and he was fined. (In 2007 a man who had taken a motorcycle from the wreck of the *Napoli* off the coast of Devon also claimed it was a souvenir, he wasn't believed either!)

Wrecking can still take place today and many people still seem to believe that something washed ashore belongs to whoever finds it. In 1999 a sailing event in Weymouth Bay almost turned to tragedy. The organisers had ignored warnings and allowed the event to take place when squalls were expected. A sudden violent squall capsized 77 two man catamarans. Happily the rescue boats saved all the people and only one woman needed hospital treatment. The vessels were washed up all around Weymouth Bay and as far east as Durdle Door. By the time some of these were recovered fittings had been removed. The wreckers were still at work.

4: Coastal Defence – Against Enemies

The Bulbury Anchor, the oldest anchor ever found in Britain. Dating from the beginning of the first millennium and discovered in a hill-fort near Wareham, it bears out Julius Caesar's description of the strong and seaworthy vessels of the late Iron Age.

COASTAL DEFENCE CAN HAVE TWO MEANINGS: the coast can be defended against the action of the sea, and also against human attack. In both cases the geology and form of the coast can affect the vulnerability of the coast to attack, and for the most part the coast has protected Dorset from human invasion. It is impossible, or very difficult, to land on most of the coast, the only accessible points have long been developed as harbours, and these have a long history of defence. In addition attacks have taken place on the sea and defences against enemy raiders, or pirates, taking local vessels, were in many cases, of equal importance to the local population.

Probably as long as people have been sailing, then ships have been used to move troops, attack enemy tribes, or carry out pirate raids. When Julius Caesar reached the Channel in about 50 BC he found the local ships more than a match for the Roman warships, and could only defeat them by landing and attacking their ports. This, together with the massive defences of Hengistbury Head at the entrance to Christchurch Harbour, the hill-fort of Flowers Barrow which dominates Worbarrow Bay or the earthworks on Bindon Hill which surrounds and defends Lulworth Cove, all suggest a prehistoric maritime world which was far from peaceful.

There is no physical or documentary evidence for any violence associated with the Roman invasion. The Romans followed a well known route to Poole Harbour and built a small fort at Hamworthy. This seems to have been more to house the troops organising the off loading of supplies rather than to overawe or oppress the local population, as it clearly had a limited life. As the focus of the invasion moved north and west the fort fell into disuse. Within a few years the ditches were being used to make salt and the sword had been turned into a ploughshare.

Three hundred years later Roman Britain itself came under attack from Saxon raiders in the east and Irish raiders in the west, but there seems to have been little military activity in Dorset. There have been claims of Roman 'watch towers', set up as a defence against such incursions. However none of these has ever been proved by excavation. Whenever any of the so called watch towers has been excavated it has turned out to be something very different. When the Saxons did arrive it was by land rather than water, and the Saxon 'invasion' was far from successful. Dorset was surrounded and absorbed by the Saxon kingdoms rather than conquered.

It is the Saxon kingdom of Wessex, that faced the most serious maritime attacks that have, in fact, ever been recorded for Dorset. It began with a minor incident recorded in the Anglo-Saxon Chronicle for 787:

> [Then] came [the] first three ships of the Northmen from the land of robbers. The reeve then rode thereto, and would take them to the king's town [Dorchester] ; for he knew not what they were; and there was he slain. These were the first ships of the Danish men that sought the land of the English nation.

Some people have doubted that this event ever took place, claiming that it was added to enhance the importance of Wessex, where the Chronicle, was written. However in the year 800 it is recorded that the northern shores of France were harassed by the Northmen, and that they had been attacking it for some years previously. So it is possible that the marauders of 787 was a ship that had come across the Channel, perhaps separated from the main raiding party.

England soon faced almost continuous attacks by the Vikings, mostly in the north, but in 836

> This year fought King Egbert with thirty-five pirates [ships] at Charmouth, where a great slaughter was made, and the Danes remained masters of the field.

And again in 840

> Alderman Ethelhelm with the men of Dorsetshire, fought with the Danish army in Portland-isle, and for a good while put them to flight; but in the end the Danes became masters of the field, and slew the alderman.

It has been claimed, but with no real evidence, that there is one surviving relic of these battles, in the shrine of St Wite at Whitchurch Canonicorum. One tradition has it that she was an anchoress (female hermit) killed by a party of raiding Vikings. All that is certain is that the bones of a small woman were found inside her shrine when it was opened in 1900, preserved in a damaged lead casket bearing the inscription;

✠hICREꝖESCT·RELIꝖE·SCE·WITE

HIC REꝖESCT RELIꝖE SCTE WITE [Here rest the remains of St Wite]

By the end of the ninth century things were getting much worse. In 876

> This year the army stole into Wareham, a fort of the West-Saxons. The king afterwards made peace with them; and they gave him as hostages those who

The Shrine of St Wite at Whitchurch Canonicorum. A plausible local legend is that she was an anchorite killed by Vikings.

The inscription found on the lead reliquary inside the shrine. The legend reads, 'hic reqesct reliqe scte wite' – Here rest the remains of St Wite.

were worthiest in the army; and swore with oaths on the holy bracelet, which they would not before to any nation, that they would readily go out of his kingdom. Then, under colour of this, their cavalry stole by night into Exeter.

A.D. 877. This year came the Danish army into Exeter from Wareham; whilst the navy sailed west about, until they met with a great mist at sea, and there perished one hundred and twenty ships at Swanage.

Victorian Swanage had a fascination with the Vikings and at the end of the nineteenth century George Burt, a prominent local businessmen, erected a memorial to the events of 877 on the sea front.

Amongst other litter in [George Burt's yard] there would seem to have been some cannon balls. He seems to have had some difficulty in working these in for the adornment of his birthplace. Cannon balls suggest a battle, but there had been no battle at Swanage. King Alfred however is supposed to have defeated the Danes in Swanage Bay in the year of our Lord 877. Naturally enough the contractor erected a pillar on the Marine Parade to commemorate this proud if dim event, and placed the cannon balls on top of it. To some these missiles may seem inappropriate, as gun powder was not invented until more than 400 years after the assumed engagement.

Five miles west of Swanage along the coast, lies Winspit where there are numerous old coastal quarries. At the entrance to the short galleries there are numerous simple carvings of various sailing ships. Most are of vessels that could have been seen in the nineteenth century sailing along the channels, indeed the majority are of ships which carried the quarried stone to London. However one is very different. It shows a fantastic vessel with a single mast ship, with a square sail and pennant, as well as dragon figure head and what appears to be a ram. Probably this ship is supposed to be a Viking ship, and it was seen in Swanage, but not in the ninth century but the nineteenth, during a Victorian summer regatta! Indeed it is easy to imagine such an 'event', Vikings (undoubtedly wearing hairy cloaks and horned helmets) coming ashore from a fishing boat dressed up for the occasion, to fight with a group of 'Saxons' and probably carry off a struggling maiden or two.

This romantic version can obscure the terrible reality that the Viking raids were. Evidence for the impact of the raids can be seen in the town of Wareham, which was the principal Dorset port at the time, an obvious target for Viking attacks. It was therefore an obvious town to be defended as one of King Alfred's new 'Burghs' (fortified strongpoints), part of a wider military defence strategy that Alfred developed and which kept Wessex safe for a hundred years. The massive earthen ramparts which were built on Alfred's orders still surround the town, mute evidence of both Alfred's brilliance as a military leader and the threat which he had to face.

A hundred years later the Vikings returned and this time it was even worse, there were attacks on Devon, Cornwall and Hampshire and in

A.D. 982 In this year came up in Dorsetshire three ships of the pirates, and plundered in Portland. The same year London was burned.

A.D. 998 This year coasted the army back eastward into the mouth of the

The Viking memorial on Swanage sea front. There probably was no naval victory but it was a good way of using up some stone cannon balls.

Frome, and went up everywhere, as widely as they would, into Dorsetshire. Often was an army collected against them; but, as soon as they were about to come together, then were they ever through something or other put to flight, and their enemies always in the end had the victory. Another time they lay in the Isle of Wight, and fed themselves meanwhile from Hampshire and Sussex.

In 2009 an amazing discovery was made near Weymouth which probably relates to one of these raids on southern England.

Archaeologists working on the Weymouth Relief Road discovered a burial pit of dismembered skeletons on Ridgeway Hill. Fifty-one decapitated skulls were found in one distinct area of the pit and fifty four bodies were found randomly placed in another section of the pit. The remains were radio-carbon dated to between AD910 and AD1030, all the remains were be male and most are aged from their late teens to about 25 years old, with just a small number of older individuals. As a general group they are tall, robust in stature with good teeth. The lack of any other finds, such as those associated with clothing, indicates that they may have been naked when thrown into the pit.

Remains of ten individuals from the execution pit were analysed, the isotope results from the men's teeth show that they grew up in countries where the climate is colder than in Britain, with one individual thought to be from north of the Arctic Circle. Others had eaten a high protein based diet, comparable with known sites in Sweden. They were Vikings .

These raids were now fought on a different scale, with a bigger prize in view. In 1015 Canute attacked southern England, landing on Brownsea Island and raiding deep into Dorset. In 1017 Edmund Ironside, the English king died leaving Canute king of England.

The concept of fortified strong points to protect vulnerable locations, and act as a base for troops to fight off raiding parties, continued after the Norman Conquest. Castles were built at three important locations along the coast – Christchurch, Wareham and at Church Ope Cove on Portland, in addition Corfe Castle, though inland, served much the same purpose and acted as a base to protect the valuable Isle of Purbeck.

Christchurch and Wareham Castles were placed in important towns. Little now remains of Wareham Castle, only the motte (mound) on which the keep stood, although the

The 'Viking' graffiti in the quarry at Winspit.

Christchurch Castle and the Constable's House, lie beside the River Avon, below the Priory Church.

foundations of the massive walls of the keep survive underground. In Christchurch both fragments of the keep survive on the motte whilst the great hall survives almost intact. Sir Arthur Conan Doyle, in his historical novel *The White Company*, gives an imaginative, if not particularly accurate, description of Christchurch Castle in its heyday:

> Black was the mouth of Twynham Castle, though a pair of torches, burning at the further end of the gateway cast a red glare over the outer bailey, and sent a dim ruddy flicker through the rough-hewn arch, rising and falling with fitful brightness. Over the door the travellers could discern the escutcheon of the Montacutes, a roebuck gules on a field argent, flanked on either side by smaller shields which bore the red roses of the veteran constable. As they passed over the drawbridge, Alleyne marked the gleam of arms in the embrasures to right and left, and they had scarce set foot upon the causeway ere a hoarse blare burst from a bugle, and, with screech of hinge and clank of chain, the ponderous bridge swung up into the air, drawn by unseen hands. At the same instant the huge portcullis came rattling down from above, and shut off the last fading light of day. Sir Nigel and his lady walked on in deep talk, while a fat under-steward took charge of the three comrades, and led them to the buttery, where beef, bread, and beer were kept ever in readiness for the wayfarer. After a hearty meal and a dip in the trough to wash the dust from them, they strolled forth into the bailey, where the bowman peered about through the darkness at wall and at keep, with the carping eyes of one who has seen something of sieges, and is not lightly to be satisfied. To Alleyne and to John, however, it appeared to be as great and as stout a fortress as could be built by the hands of man.
>
> Erected by Sir Baldwin de Bedvers in the old fighting days of the twelfth century, when men thought much of war and little of comfort, Castle Twynham had been designed as a stronghold pure and simple, unlike those later and more magnificent' structures where warlike strength had been combined with the magnificence of a palace. From the time of the Edwards such buildings as Conway or Caernarvon Castles, to say nothing of Royal Windsor, had shown that it was possible to secure luxury in peace as well as security in times of trouble. Sir Nigel's trust, however, still frowned above the smooth-flowing waters of the Avon very much as the stem race of early Anglo-Normans had designed it. There were the broad outer and inner

The Constable's House, before it was cleared of ivy, one of the best preserved Norman houses in England.

baileys, not paved, but sown with grass to nourish the sheep and cattle which might be driven in on sign of danger. All round were high and turreted walls, with at the corner a bare square-faced keep, gaunt and windowless, rearing up from a lofty mound, which made it almost inaccessible to an assailant. Against the bailey-walls were rows of frail wooden houses and leaning sheds, which gave shelter to the archers and men-at-arms who formed the garrison. The doors of these humble dwellings were mostly open, and against the yellow glare from within Alleyne could see the bearded fellows cleaning their harness, while their wives would come out for a gossip, with their needle-work in their hands, and their long black shadows streaming across the yard. The air was full of the clack of their voices and the merry prattling of children, in strange contrast to the flash of arms and constant warlike challenge from the walls above.

"Methinks a company of school lads could hold this place against an army," quoth John.

"And so say I," said Alleyne.

"Nay, there you are wide of the clout," the bowman said gravely. "By my hilt! I have seen a stronger fortalice carried in a summer evening. I remember such a one in Picardy, with a name as long as a Gascon's pedigree.

Indeed both Wareham and Christchurch Castles are not well situated to provide protection from a maritime enemy. At Wareham an enemy coming up the Frome would come to the town first, then the castle, whilst at Christchurch there is the rich abbey lying between the Castle and the quays. Only at Portland is the castle (known as Rufus or Bow and Arrow Castle) situated in a position to deter raiders, above the only landing place on the island at Church Ope. No trace now remains of this castle, the present building dates from the late fifteenth century and may not even be on the same site.

In 1340 the French attacked Portland. It is not known what, if any, resistance to this raid was given by Rufus Castle. These raids, of which this is one of the earliest, were one aspect of the Anglo-French wars of the fourteenth and fifteenth centuries. French ships would land on the coast, a town would be attacked, looted and damaged as much as possible then the enemy would retreat, frequently before any counter attack could be organised.

Studland, Swanage, Whitecliff, and Herston were attacked in 1339 and, as already mentioned, Portland in the following year. These raids could easily ruin the local economy. In 1348 Bindon Abbey was practically bankrupt, and this was attributed to the losses caused

The ruins of Christchurch Castle, as seen from the Constable's House.

by the enemy's raids. In 1377 the French launched a series of raids along the south coast of England, Lyme Regis, and Poole were attacked whilst Melcombe Regis was 'burnt and destroyed.'

This type of warfare was not, of course, one sided. English vessels also raided the French coast, in a tit-for-tat fashion. In 1404 the French attacked Portland, this time the local population fought back, the enemy were prevented from returning to their ships and, aided by men from the mainland, many of the enemy were killed or captured. The following year the English retaliated and burnt forty Norman towns and villages.

The French retaliated in kind in the autumn of 1405. This raid is remarkable, not for the damage it caused but because a first hand account of the attack on Poole survives, from the French side!

Three Spanish and two French galleys, under Don Pedro Nino and Charles de Savoisi, sailed in August. After raiding Cornwall and Devon they made Portland, where they met with little resistance.

> On coming into the neighbourhood of Poole Harbour, Pero Nino no sooner heard that he was near 'Arripay's' [Harry Paye, Poole Privateer] place of abode, than he determined to return the visits which that corsair, had paid to the Spanish coast. Accordingly they entered the harbour, and came at day-break in sight of Poole. The town was not walled; and there was a handsome tower with a cupola. Here the French commander thought it would be rash to attempt a landing; and when the Spaniard, as if the honour of his country required him to take some vengeance here, persisted in his purpose, Mosen Charles forbade any of his people to land with him. The Spaniards landed under the command of Pedro's kinsman, Fernando Nino, with orders not to encumber themselves with plunder, but to plant their banner before the place, and set the houses on fire. One large building was maintained awhile against them; but when, after a stout resistance, they forced an entrance, the defendants escaped at the back part; and here the invaders found arms and sea stores of all kinds: they carried off what they could, and then set the storehouse on fire. By this time, the English had collected, in some force, archers and men at arms; and having put themselves in array, they came so near, that it might well be seen who was of a ruddy complexion, and who of a dark one. They had taken the doors out of the houses, which they contrived, by means of supports, to place before them as pavaises, to protect them against the cross-bow shot. Under this cover, the archers kept up a brisk discharge with such effect that the arbalisters dared not expose themselves while they stooped to charge their arbalists. Many were wounded, and those whose armour protected them, are described as fledged with arrows. Pedro Nino, seeing his people in danger, and that they were beginning to fall back, landed with the rest of his men; and the French then, notwithstanding their previous determination, hastened with all speed, like brave men, to support him. He set up the cry of " Santiago ! Santiago !" and the English, who fought right well, were at length compelled to retreat, leaving among the slain, a brother of Arripay's, a gallant man of arms, who distinguished himself by his great exertions before he fell. They then retired to their vessels, and proceeded towards Southampton.

Portland was attacked again in 1416, and in 1439 or 40 Bexington, near Abbotsbury, is reported to have been attacked. This raid, small though it was, left one of the only visible

COASTAL DEFENCE – AGAINST ENEMIES

reinforcements of seamen were put ashore. The admiral was off Lyme on 23 May, and found four vessels already in the anchorage from which powder and provisions had been landed. When Warwick arrived the garrison was in sore need, but corn and powder were sent ashore and the sailors of the squadron added fish and bread saved out of their rations, with shoes and clothes from their kits for the ragged and bare-footed men at the front. The squadron took part in the operations by sending the ships' boats along the coast towards Bridport, landing in the enemy's rear and thus diverting his attention. In the town men and women — the latter filled the soldiers' bandoliers while they fought — were equally undaunted; but when Prince Maurice drew off on 15 June it was because the fleet had enabled them to hold out for the coming of the army of relief under the Earl of Essex.

As the Civil War was coming to an end, a new enemy appeared. Now the British were fighting the Dutch. Most of the fighting was in distant corners of the world, or at sea. One of the main sea battles of the war was the second Battle of Portland. On 18 February 1653 the Dutch Admiral Maarten Tromp, who was trying to protect a convoy of homeward bound Dutch merchantmen, attacked an English Fleet off Portland. The numbers of warships were about equal and the Dutch were in high spirits having defeated an English fleet at Dungeness the previous year. However during the winter the admiralty under Sir Henry Vane had devised a new formation, line of battle. This formation was to dominate naval warfare for the next two hundred years. The Dutch fleet fought hard but couldn't counter the new tactics. The battle lasted until 20 February. During it the English lost two ships and three were badly damaged, the Dutch lost at least nine warships and between thirty and forty merchantmen. The war had been turned in England's favour.

For the next hundred and fifty years, whilst Britain was often at war, the main battles generally took place a long way away. The chief anxiety on the coast now related not to the enemy's fleets but to his privateers. Some of the stories told of them were amazing:

> In 1694, Capt. Peter Jolliffe, of Poole, who was cruising in a small hoy, called the "Sea Adventure," perceiving a French privateer off the Isle of Purbeck, make a prize of a fishing boat belonging to Weymouth, boldly attacked the privateer, though of three times his strength, and having first obliged him to quit his prize, afterwards forced him on shore, near the village of Lulworth, the people of which made themselves masters of the vessel, and took the crew prisoners. For this brave exploit, captain Jolliffe was honoured with a

A Victorian view of the Battle of Portland.

magnificent gold chain and medal, presented to him by the king with the following inscription :

"His Mates' Gift as a Reward to PETER JOLLIF, of Poole, for his good Service against the Enemy in retaking a Ketch of Weymouth from a French Privateer, and chaceing the said Privateer on Shoar near Lulworth in ye Isle of Purbeck, where shee was broken in peeces. 1694."

The honourable reward bestowed in this instance appears to have acted as a wholesome stimulus, for a still more daring action was undertaken on the 30th of May, 1695, by William Thompson, master of a fishing boat, belonging to Poole, who, when fishing near the Isle of Purbeck, accompanied by only one man and a boy, perceived a privateer of Cherbourg bearing down upon him. He was so far from avoiding the enemy that he made ready to defend himself the best way he could, with two little guns which he had mounted and some small arms; and with so inconsiderable a force he behaved himself with such success that in a little time he wounded the captain the lieutenant, and six more of the French, which so discouraged the rest that they bore away. But then, in his turn, Thompson, encouraged by the success of his valour, gave chase to the privateer, fired upon her incessantly for two hours, and at length made the enemy strike, beg for quarter, and surrender; so that Thompson, thus victorious, brought away the sloop with fourteen prisoners, of whom the captain was one, having left two more at Corfe Castle, and brought her into Poole Harbour. This privateer had two pateraroes, several small arms and grenadoes, and sixteen men. For this gallant proceeding the lords of the admiralty gave Thompson not only the vessel he had taken, but a gold chain and medal, similar to that presented to captain Jolliffe.

This was celebrated in a street ballad (the spelling has been modernised)

THE COURAGIOUS CAPTAIN,
OR

A brief account of the several noble attempts and valiant exploits performed by the honoured captain Peter Jolliffe over the French Privateers to his unspeakable praise, and the honour of the Kingdom, in general tune of Captain Hastins, or, the serious Lover.

Right valiant Thomson, brave and bold,
a medal had and chain of gold
for taking a French privateer;
but now another captain hear

Hath since receiv'd the same reword,
for noble actions don one board,
deserving more then common fame,
stout Peter Jolliffe called by name.

He more than once or twice did fight,
and put French privateers to flight,

as by the sequel you shall find,
which shows his bold undaunted mind.

Now while he ploughed the ocean wide,
the privateers at length he spied,
whom he did charge with might and main
till he retook that ship again.

One of the privateers he chased,
who for to save their lines in haste
did to the nearest shore repair,
but Peter catched them napping there.

Then without any more ado,
the monsieur captain and his crew,
stout Peter Jolliffe took that day,
and brought them close confined away.

For this brave valiant act, behold,
he has receiv'd a chain of gold,
a medal and commission too,
that he the French may still pursue.

Let their renowned actions be
recorded to posterity,
that others, hearing of their fame,
may strive to imitate the same.

It might seem surprising that a fishing boat would be armed, but the threat of privateers was very real and slight resistance might be enough to enable a vessel to escape. There is physical evidence of this. Just east of Portland lies the wreck of one of the vessels engaged in the stone trade, she sank in about 1730 and amongst some of the objects archaeologists found on board were musket balls.

Whilst naval ships and British privateers provided some protection on sea the anchorages also needed protection. This was provided by a series of batteries along the coast.

Taylor's map of Dorset of 1765 shows batteries on Peverel and Handfast Points, at North and South Haven Points (each four guns), and at Poole Head. At Weymouth the fort under the Nothe is shown.

The Napoleonic War led to a change in policy. Some of the batteries were not renewed (as usual during periods of peace, defences were allowed to decay), but replaced with signal stations. Those at Ballard Hill, Round Down, St Aldhelm's Head, Hamborough Hill, the Verne, Portland, Puncknowle, and Whitelands date from 1794, and Golden Cap from 1796. In 1803 a return was made to the mediaeval system of fire beacons which were prepared for use in suitable positions.

At Portland Castle there were five cannons, but with two detached batteries mounting seven guns between them. At Swanage there was a powder magazine and a three gun battery. The Nothe Fort at Weymouth consisted of a central circular building of brick for two traversing guns, with platforms on either flank carrying two guns each and Bridport possessed two batteries, of two guns each.

Across the county was a network of beacons, which were an impressive statement of defence for, by the beginning of the nineteenth century, invasion was again possible. Beacons were erected on carefully chosen locations, local landowners would organise the manning of the beacon and later be reimbursed from central funds. For example the receipt for the manning of the beacon on Black Down above Portesham survives:

> To Mr Joseph Hardy
> Portesham
> Sir
> I am directed by Lord Dorchester to desire that you will without delay, send me an account of the whole expense of erecting, and also watching the beacon on Blagdon [Black Down] Hill from the beginning to the present time according to the form below, in order that the same may be discharged forthwith.
> Edward Boswell
> Clerk to the Lieutenancy
> May 2nd
> Received of Mr Hardy £1, 16s for attending to the beacon four weeks at 9s a week.
> William Boyt X his mark."

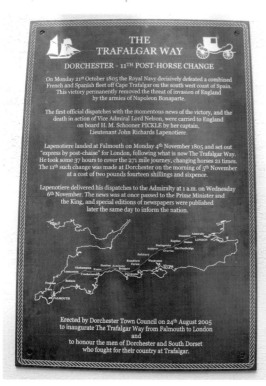

After the Battle of Trafalgar the news was brought by HMS *Pickle* to Falmouth, then the Lieut Lapenotiere travelled to London overland. In 2005 the journey was re-enacted and plaques were erected along the route.

This beacon was on property owned by Captain Thomas Hardy, friend of Admiral Nelson and Captain of HMS *Victory* at the battle of Trafalgar. The battle had a great impact in Dorset as there were men from the county in almost all of the ships which took part. Some were famous, apart from Hardy. There was the lucky Henry Digby who not only sailed unscathed through Trafalgar but made over £40000 in prize money during the war (many millions today), and Charles Bullen who was the scourge of the slave trade and was responsible for freeing over 10000 Africans and later designed Queen Victoria's first Royal Yacht. All in all there were 186 men from Dorset who served at Trafalgar.

As news of the victory at Trafalgar spread there was widespread celebration, muted by the knowledge of Nelson's death. The celebrations at Burton Bradstock were particularly notable, where the villagers took a personal interest in the outcome of the battle. The son of their leading citizen, the twenty year old Richard Francis Roberts was a midshipman on board HMS *Victory*. The news of the battle reached Burton before it even reached London, as Lieutenant Lapenotiere passed through Bridport, bringing news of the victory to the capital. One of the letters sent to Richard Roberts takes up the story.

> We first heard of the engagement on the morning of the 5th Nov. The account was sent by Mr. J. Hounsell to Burton soon after Lieutenant Lapinoture [sic] passed Bridport. It informed us of the death of Lord Nelson; and that 19 ships were taken and one blown up. Our feelings were extremely racked; all deploring the loss of the Hero; all measurably pleased the victory was so decisively in our favour. But at the same time our minds were much distressed on your account. For my own part I never experienced

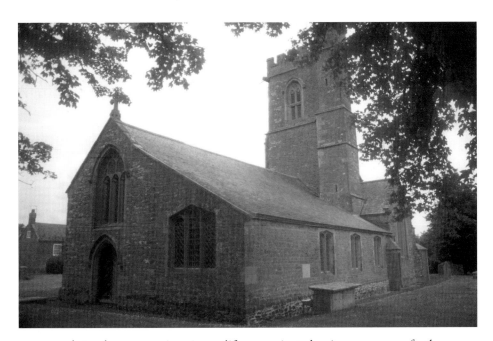

The church at
Burton Bradstock,
where the drunken
bell ringers rang so
hard to celebrate
victory at Trafalgar
that they broke the
bell ropes.

such incoherent emotions in my life; one minute hoping you were safe; the
next doubting it from the dreadful carnage that was inevitable in such a
situation. From this dilemma nothing could relieve me but hearing
immediately from you. Every post was looked for, with indescribable anxiety
[which] was not dispelled till the receipt of your very acceptable letter dated
Oct 22nd &&. The bells rang till several of the ropes broke! They were
repaired next morning. Your father's colours were hoisted on the [church]
tower and continued flying several days.

Whilst his younger brother adds more details of the celebration:

We had bell ringing and beer drinking the night & when we received your
letter. The colours were hoisted from the tower. Mother had hard work to
keep the beer barrell [sic] a running. We gave away beer to almost every man
in the parish. I was almost drunk myself.

The scenes at Burton Bradstock were repeated all over the country. All classes rejoiced in
the news, from the squire knowing that his son was safe, to the drunken bell ringer in the
church tower, breaking the ropes in his enthusiasm. All rejoiced in the news of the victory
since it had ended the threat of French invasion for ever, but their enthusiasm was muted
by the knowledge that Britain had lost one of its greatest heroes. As *The Times* put it:

We know not whether to mourn or rejoice. The country has gained the most
splendid and decisive Victory that has ever graced the naval annals of
England: but it has been dearly purchased. *The great and gallant Nelson is no more.*

One group who were very much affected by the victory were the Burton Volunteers. All
around the coast volunteer regiments were established, a form of Home Guard, to fight the
French if they landed. The Burton Volunteers were very proud of their regiment, and
considered it the best in Dorset. A song, first recorded in 1807, celebrates the brave
volunteers of Burton, and was doubtless sung by the revellers as they celebrated the victory
at Trafalgar.

THE SONG OF THE BURTON VOLUNTEERS
Come, my lads of courage true,
Ripe for martial glory,
See the Standard waves for you,
And leads the way before ye.
Chorus -
To the field of Mars advance,
Join the bold alliance;
Tell the blood-stained sons of France,
We bid them all defiance.

Burton's sons were always brave
On the land or ocean
Ready for to kill or save
Where honour's the promotion.
Chorus

Burton long has had a boast,
And right well deserving;
For pretty maids a standing toast
Of nature's sweet preserving.
Chorus

Gallia's sons invasion plans
Threat'ning to destroy us,
Seize our maidens, houses, lands,
And as slaves employ us.
Chorus

We must fight, or starve, or fly,
Hope nought else remaining;
or wives may faint and children die
With no hand sustaining.
Final Chorus -
Lives are lent for Laws and King,
When that they may need'em;
Let us then in chorus sing,
Give us death or freedom.

When Admiral Thomas Hardy died in 1839 it was decided to erect a memorial to him in Dorset, and it was decided to place it on land he had owned close to the site of the beacon on Blackdown. Paid for by public subscription, the foundation stone was laid on 21 October 1844, Trafalgar Day.

A plaque on the north side reads:

Erected by public subscription
In Memory of
Vice Admiral Sir Thomas Masterman Hardy Bart. GCB
Flag Captain to Lord Nelson
On HMS Victory at the Battle of Trafalgar

Restored 1900
And placed in charge of the National Trust
For Places of Historic Interest and Natural Beauty
By the descendants of Sir Thomas Masterman Hardy

The Hardy Monument is still a popular tourist attraction, and, which the Admiral would have liked, it is marked on the charts as a seamark.

From the late eighteenth century onwards several people had proposed building a breakwater to enclose all or part of the anchorage at Portland. This idea was controversial, not only would it be very expensive but some people thought it would ruin the anchorage! In fact they had a point, a south west wind blowing across Chesil Beach (and this is the commonest direction for the wind to blow) would naturally push any ship in the harbour onto any breakwater. When there were only sailing ships this was a real problem, even when ships were steam powered there were problems, as if the boilers were cold (common enough in a harbour) the ship had no steam and hence no power. If something goes wrong with the mooring the ship could be driven by the wind onto the breakwater. Indeed this happened and thirty one ships have been wrecked on the breakwater, all on the inside exactly where the sceptics of the early nineteenth century said they would.

It was nervousness on the part of the British Government that finally led to the building of the breakwater as in the 1840s the French began to fortify Cherbourg, on the opposite side of the Channel. This was seen as a real threat to Britain. France was seen as the natural enemy and there was concern that there was no strong point to counter Cherbourg between Plymouth and Portsmouth.

Work began in August, 1847, first under J. M. Rendel and then Sir John Coode, the first stone was laid (in fact lowered into the sea) by Prince Albert on 25 July 1849. This visit is mentioned in passing by Thomas Hardy in *The Mayor of Casterbridge*:

> A Royal Personage was about to pass through the borough, on his course further west, to inaugurate an immense engineering work out that way. He had consented to halt half-an-hour or so in the town, and to receive an address from the corporation of Casterbridge, which, as a representative centre of husbandry, wished thus to express its sense of the great services he had rendered to agricultural science and economics, by his zealous promotion of designs for placing the art of farming on a more scientific footing.

The Victorians were fascinated by the great engineering projects of the day, and would regard them as tourist attractions. The breakwater under construction was just such an attraction. In 1858 Charles Dickens visited Portland and wrote an article about the island for his magazine, *Household Words*. As well as the other visitor attractions he gives a detailed description of the breakwater under construction.

> We land from the steamer about midway between the breakwater and the shingly isthmus. Turning to the left from the end of the small pier, a quarter of a mile of road skirting the beach, and flanked on the right by the slope of underlying clay which forms the base of Portland, we come to the entrance gate of the Works. Names must be entered here in the visitor's book; two melancholy policemen narrowly eye our method of penmanship and eagerly peruse names and addresses when our backs are turned. We walk forward at once towards the huge staging. A good railed passage is provided, leading

Building the
Portland Breakwater
in 1871, the wooden
platform carrying the
railway along the
breakwater can
clearly be seen.

Building the
Portland Breakwater
in 1871, the wooden
platform carrying the
railway along the
breakwater can
clearly be seen.

between two of the five broad-gauge roads which run to the end of the inner
breakwater abreast over open rafters. The large blocks of heaped stone, which
at first underlie the rafters, soon, become dashed with surf, and then give
way entirely to the sea, which, if the day be at all fresh, will give the visitor a
sprinkling. Six hundred yards from the shore the inner breakwater ends in a
noble bastion-like head, rising, with smooth round sides, some thirty feet
above the waves. A space of four hundred feet separates this head from its
partner, the precisely similar work at the end of the outer breakwater

It is a scene of bustle. Here, we pass a gang of men preparing timber for
the shores and brackets that support the road-pieces; there, we see a man
running along the narrow footway of the workmen — a single plank laid on
each side of the rails — as much at ease as if a false step would not tumble
him thirty feet down into the sea, or, worse, upon the rugged rubbly heap;
which, now emerging from the waves, indicates what the nature of this outer
arm is hereafter to be.

Every two or three minutes comes rumbling behind us a train, with its
four loaded wagons, each wagon averaging twelve tons in weight. An ordinary
load consists of a large block in the center, some two or three feet in diameter,
around which are heaped fragments of smaller sizes, the whole rising to a

The great Victorian
harbour of Portland.

The Dock Yards, Portland. W 6347.

Portland Harbour in
the nineteenth
century.

considerable height in the wagon. It is a fine thing to watch the tipping of
the rubble through the open rafters of the cage. Every wagon has a dropping-
floor, slanting downwards from back to front, but with its iron-work lighter
and less massive in front than behind. It is so contrived that a brakeman,
with a few blows of his hammer, knocks away the check, and sets the floor
free to drop; the front drops at once, because, owing to its greater depth, it
is pressed by the greater weight of stone; the whole mass tumbles with a
confused uproar upon the rubble-heap below, and then the heavy iron-work
behind causes the floor at once to return to its natural position, in which it
is immediately re-fastened. A puff or two of the engine brings each wagon
in succession over the required spot; and, unless the large stone should
become jammed, the whole load is tipped, and the empty train is on its way
back, in less than a minute.

The original breakwater was completed in 1872, the final stone being laid by the Prince of
Wales. It carried the inscription:

FROM THIS SPOT

ON THE 25TH OF JULY 1849

HIS ROYAL HIGHNESS PRINCE ALBERT

CONSORT OF QUEEN VICTORIA

SANK THE FIRST STONE OF THIS BREAKWATER

UPON THE SAME SPOT

ALBERT EDWARD. PRINCE OF WALES .

ON THE 18TH OF AUGUST 1872.

LAID THIS LAST STONE

AND DECLARED THE WORK COMPLETE.

"THESE ARE IMPERIAL WORKS

AND WORTHY KINGS"

The last line is a very apt quote from Alexander Pope's, 'Epistle To Richard Boyle, Earl of
Burlington'.

> Bid harbours open, public ways extend,
> Bid temples, worthier of the God, ascend;
> Bid the broad arch the dang'rous flood contain,
> The mole projected break the roaring main;

Back to his bounds their subject sea command,
And roll obedient rivers through the land;
These honours, peace to happy Britain brings,
These are imperial works, and worthy kings.

The breakwater, originally consisted of two arms, with an opening between them, protecting the anchorage from the south east, with forts at the ends of both arms, the most substantial at the end of the outer arm. There was then a gap of over two miles of open water to the Nothe at Weymouth. This allowed for sailing vessels to manoeuvre easily in and out of the harbour.

As well as the forts on the breakwater there was a series of other defences planned around the harbour. In 1860 work began on the Verne Citadel, high up on the northern bluff of Portland, and the Nothe Fort on the site of an ancient battery, which had first been fortified in the reign of Henry VIII. These were completed in 1872 at the same time as the breakwater. Below the Verne, on the east side of the hill, but still above the breakwater were the East Weir batteries. These completed the defences of the harbour, and were seen as state of the art – for about twenty years.

By the end of the century steel warships, fully steam powered and armed with torpedoes as well as guns meant that the harbour was vulnerable again. By now it was too important to the navy so work began on the second phase of the breakwater.

In 1895 work started on the new breakwaters, running out from Bincleaves on the mainland. By 1906 they were complete, enclosing what was then the largest artificial harbour in the world.

The defences were also upgraded, with new guns at the Nothe and Breakwater Forts. The massive iron breech blocks of the guns on the breakwater were too heavy to remove and were just dumped – they still lie there. New forts were built. Beside the Verne Citadel was the High Angle Battery, completed in 1892: shells would be fired over the cliff to sink enemy ships by plunging fire. A new fort was built at Blacknor on the western side of the island. Completed in 1901 it protected the 'backdoor' of the naval base. Finally a fort was built at Upton on the far side of Weymouth Bay. The location of this fort was chosen in an unusual fashion.

We … rented a small house at Upton near Ringstead Bay. It was a beautiful situation commanding the whole of Weymouth Bay, with woods and a small stream below. Battleships coming out of Portland Harbour were constantly practising gunnery in the bay in front of us.

One day a live shell fell about 200 yards from the house and exploded, making a huge hole in the ground. A boat's crew came ashore, with a note from the Captain apologising for the 'unfortunate incident', as well he might.

The navy said it was an isolated incident, then the following year:

Three more shells fell in an adjoining field and woods … one flew over a small bungalow, a little girl passing through the wood on a public path, heard one hissing over her head and saw it fall and roll through the trees not far from her.

The Admiralty apologised again, issued orders to prevent firing onshore, but then:

A few years later we were turned out of our house by the War Office, who

HMS Hood, towed
into position in the
southern entrance to
Portland Harbour.

As she sank she
turned turtle, she
still lies there.

wanted to build a fort on the site, corresponding to that at the end of the
breakwater, so as to command the entrance to the harbour on both side.

These defences were seen as adequate during the First World War, apart from one change
made to the breakwater. It was realised that the southern entrance, though well defended
by mid nineteenth century standards could not easily be defended against attack by
torpedoes and torpedo boats. The easiest and quickest way to seal the entrance was to sink
a block-ship. What they used was an obsolete battleship.

The first HMS *Hood* was a 380 foot long, 14000 ton battleship built in 1891. At this
time warship design was very fluid as naval architects tried to create the ideal battleship. This
wasn't achieved until *Dreadnought* ten years later. The *Hood* was very much a test piece, and
an unsuccessful one. Her heavy armour and low freeboard combined to make her sail very
poorly, however she looked impressive and was ideal for the role of 'showing the flag' on
the Mediterranean station where she served for nine years.

By 1914 she was obsolete and would have gone to the scrapyard, but instead she was
chosen as the block-ship. HMS *Hood* was towed out to the entrance in November 1914, the
sea cocks were opened, but difficult as ever she didn't sink fast enough, and began to drift
out of position. Then George Symonds, a professional diver in Portland Harbour, was sent

A square type 26 pillbox on Chesil Beach near Abbotsbury.

An Allan Williams Turret overlooking Worbarrow Bay.

Three Second World War coastal pillboxes, which came in a variety of forms.

Above: A round type 25 pillbox on the shore of the Fleet.

down to place explosives on the hull. This blew a hole in her hull and sank her exactly across the harbour entrance. It was intended to sink her vertically, instead she turned turtle as she sank. The officer in charge of the sinking was heard to mutter, 'a bugger to the last!'

For the rest of his life George Symonds was known as the, 'man who sank the *Hood*'.

In the Second World War invasion was a real possibility, and the coast was defended in essentially the same way as it had been when the French threatened invasion centuries earlier. Then blockhouses had been built along the coast, now the coast was to be lined with pillboxes, and anti landing traps. 'Dragons Teeth' at places where the German might land. In some places they were painted and moulded to look like beach huts. In Balaclava Bay, just outside Portland Harbour, an obvious place for a commando raid, the defence were placed underwater to catch the bottom of any incoming vessel. Then there were pillboxes and guns, all to delay any landing force. Along the coast today you can find numerous examples of pill boxes and the remains of gun emplacements, evidence of the most recent defences of the coast.

FLAME BARRAGE

Studland was the location for the trials of a potentially terrible weapon, the Flame Barrage. During the 1930s a government scientist, Donald Banks, had witnessed a shipping disaster when an oil tanker caught fire. He had been impressed by the sight of burning fuel oil spreading across the sea. He realised that if it was possible to spread oil on the sea in advance of an invading force, then set it on fire, it would prove an impenetrable defence. So was formed the idea of the Flame Barrage, which was developed by the Petroleum Warfare Department under Donald Banks. After experiments in the Solent a full sized trial was planned for Studland. Large storage tanks were built, pipes led down to the beach, an oil mixture was created and all was ready.

The first trials in December were a disaster, in front of Alexander and Montgomery – nothing happened. The mixture was too thin, it broke up on the surface and wouldn't light. However a month later it worked spectacularly, lit at night it made a mockery of the blackout in Poole and Bournemouth, Air Raid Patrol Wardens claimed that they could read a newspaper by the glare on Bournemouth sea front. Field Marshall Alexander returned a couple of weeks later and was very impressed, a barge had been moored off shore and had been completely destroyed in the inferno. Orders were given for Flame Barrages to be established at the most vulnerable places along the coast. But now the scientists were less certain, they realised that the barrage could only work in sheltered waters, so whilst barrages were established at one or two places such as Pegwell Bay in Kent, the decision was made to let the Germans know about the Flame Barrage!

The Germans at all levels had a great respect for British inventiveness so the idea that the British had discovered a way of, 'setting the sea on fire', was very believable. Rumours spread amongst the German troops gathering for the invasion, helped by some of the propaganda broadcasts from England. These purported to be German broadcasts to the troops. One contained helpful advice for the invading troops.

> The English, as you know, are notoriously bad at languages, and so it will be best, meine Herren Engellandfahrer, if you learn a few useful English phrases before the invasion.
>
> Now just repeat after me: Das Boot sinkt. The boat is sinking; the boat is sinking.
>
> Das Wasser ist kalt. The water is cold. Sehr kalt, very cold.
>
> Now, I will give you a verb that should come in useful. Again please repeat

Three circular earthworks marking the site of Cold War era radio masts on Portland Bill.

after me, Ich brenne, I burn. Du brennst, you burn. Er brennt, he burns. Wir
brennen, we burn. Ihr brennt, you are burning.

And if I may be allowed to suggest a phrase: Der SS Sturmfiihrer brennt
auch ganz schon, The SS Captain is also burning quite nicely, the SS Captain
is also burning quite nicely!

This had the desired result, after the war it was found that the rumour had been widespread
amongst the troops waiting to cross the channel, and had had a very negative (or positive
from the British point of view) effect on morale. On this side of the channel there were
rumours, which the authorities wouldn't deny, that large numbers of burnt bodies had been
washed up on a beach somewhere, or picked up by a naval vessel, whilst the only German
bodies recovered were from aircraft that had been shot down or small naval vessels that had
sunk. Many people believed (indeed some still believe) that the Germans had tried to invade
only to be beaten back by a Flame Barrage.

Incidentally there are people today who call the Flame Barrage scheme the Fougasse, but
this is simply wrong. The Fougasse was a terrestrial method of defence, essentially an
incendiary mine designed to burn vehicles, at sea it was the Flame Barrage.

Although so recent in date the Cold War has left its own legacy in the form of
monuments along the coast. Perhaps the most curious can be found on Portland Bill to the
north-west of the Lighthouse. Here aerial photographs show circular banks, for all the
world like rather neat prehistoric disc barrows. There is one problem with this, they are
very modern. If you look at the aerial photographs of the area in 1947 there is nothing
there, in 1972 one circle, in 1992 three circles and it is clear by now what they are, the base
of massive aerials. Now the aerials have gone and left earthworks behind, another layer on
the tapestry formed by the defence of the Dorset coast.

5: Coastal Defence – Against the Sea

COASTAL DEFENCE AND RECLAMATION

For the last twelve thousand years, ever since the end of the last ice age, the sea level around the Dorset coast has been rising, and the coastline has been retreating. In recent centuries the only, natural, exception to this rule has been the Studland Peninsula at the entrance to Poole Harbour. During the sixteenth century, when the first recognisable maps were produced the Studland Peninsula appears as a long narrow spit of land. The spit grew during the eighteenth century when developing sand dunes enclosed a large bay on the eastern side. In the early nineteenth century the bay was only linked to the sea at high tide, and was a favoured haunt of fishermen, wildfowlers and smugglers. By the end of the century the bay was completely cut off from the sea and is now freshwater, though still known as Little Sea.

Elsewhere erosion was the rule, and for much of the Dorset coast, for much of recorded history, there has been a continuous battle with the sea. On the one hand people living along the coast have faced the almost constant threat of coastal erosion, with their land and homes at risk of being washed away by the sea, on the other hand people have looked out at coastal marshes and land exposed at low tide and wondered if it could be won from the sea, frequently combining the two motives by winning land from the sea in order to protect land further behind. However it happed the result was always the same, land needed to be defended, as land won from the sea had to be protected. Along the Dorset the coast the battle has been going on for centuries, the more important the land was to the local community, the greater the importance given to maintaining the sea defences. The inhabitants of Romney Marsh in Kent summed this up in the rhyme.

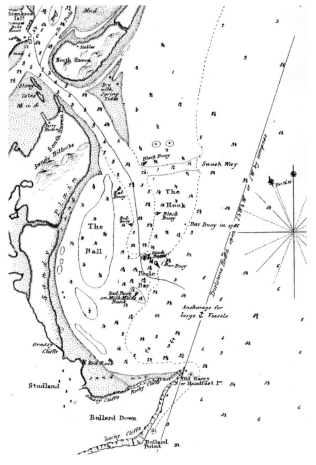

The Studland Peninsula with the brackish pool of Little Sea shown on a chart of 1825.

Praise God,
Honour the King,
But first maintain the Wall!

There is, as yet, no firm evidence of land reclamation or coastal defence during prehistoric or Roman times, though prehistoric coastal defences have been found at Hayling Island and Roman schemes on the Somerset coast. However there are some intriguing banks lying in the Moors, to the west of Arne, on the shores of Poole Harbour which are probably the remains of a very early sea wall. They predate the seventeenth century and may well be the remains of a Roman sea wall.

As early as the eighth century there is documentary evidence of both coastal erosion and land reclamation. In about 700, Aldhelm, first bishop of Sherborne, wrote a long Latin poem, known as the *Carmina Rythmicum*, in which he apparently gives a first hand account of a devastating storm. The historian Katherine Barker has made a strong case for the storm having happened at Lyme Regis.

The mighty elements and chaotic masses of the universe were driven to collision under the fiery dome of the vaulted sky.

The winds violently sweeping along the foam and surging wildly with its impetus came from the compass point where the sun sets.

The earth shuddered in discord and mighty oaks crashed down with their crowns and their roots both shattered.

Similarly the waves of the sea crash in upon the gravelly beach where the violence and aggression of the waters make their assault.

On the surface of the sea the salty waves were white-capped since the surging whirlpool was seething with wintery floods, and the ocean with its mighty strength and surging floodtide was pounding the promontories with victory near at hand. In such a way the sea swelled with the savage blasts of wind driven by its force up against the rocky shore.

When we were celebrating Matins and the psalmody of the Divine Office, suddenly with a blast of wind the pillars [of the church] trembled in their foundations then the entire wooden structure with its mighty beams shuddered and tottered, shaken in every corner of the church.

Amidst these mighty gales and tempests of terrors our hearts trembled when our eyes beheld such horrendous events. The vault of the roof was creaking with terrifying moans and groans.

At this point the congregation fleeing across the shattered vestibule finally seeks the door of the church in flight with disaster striking.

Disaster is averted through the Virgin's intervention, some flee in two bounds to the steep and slippery banks of the nearby hillside for they greatly feared that the church would be levelled by the uproar.

However when the black clouds and shadows had passed and the veil of darkness had been sundered by the brightness of the sunrise.

Then, seeing the fragments of the church roof scattered everywhere, I say; look the terrifying display of last night is now visible, here the roof beams of the church where the most glorious and sweet delight [of worship] were customarily taken have crashed to their foundations.

See here the foliage of the leafy broom basking in the sun has been blasted from the walls by the winds' battering ram.

Alas the roof's protective covering is lying all over the street.

Here look the roof thatch has collapsed leaving no defence [against the weather] These are the wanton sports of the cruel winds' blast.

Furthermore if the holy feast day of St Paul [29 June] had not been offering protection to the terrified souls of the fearful we might perhaps have been struck by lightening once the roof was shattered.

Therefore let us all snatched from danger give thanks with gratitude to the Church which reigns forever. Glory be to the unbegotten God and to the begotten son together with the Holy Ghost ruling all ages beyond.

About seventy years late, in 774, King Cynewulf of Wessex, granted an area of land at Lyme Regis to the Bishop of Sherborne for making salt:

> I King Cynewulf on the entreaty of my venerable bishop Aethelmod … to the church of Sherborne one mansio of land … next to the west bank of the river which in the vernacular is called the Lim, not very far from the place where its mouth flows into the sea; in that said place … salt is to be boiled to provide for many essential requirements be it for flavouring foodstuffs or for the divine office for use by those in authority who daily need this in the cause of Christian observance. If however it is wished to increase and to extend this donation let it be that the lord of that estate [extends his holding] on living ground. […augeat dominus locum euis in terra viventium]

The strangest phrase in this document is the reference to 'living land' (terra viventium). The most likely meaning is land that is growing, as mudflats and marshes can do at the mouth of a river. It was here, if the Bishop needed more land for salt-making he was to enclose the land. If this ever happened it would be the earliest recorded case of land reclamation in Dorset.

These documents would suggest that thirteen hundred years ago the situation of Lyme Regis was very different to today, with flat landing lying on either side of the river mouth with marshland and mudflats beyond that. It is possible that this land was protected by a ridge of land that projected into the sea to the west of the town. About eight hundred years ago this ridge was swept away, either through storms or as a result of a major landslip. The flat land at Lyme was rapidly eroded and the port devastated. It was in order to save the port and try and protect Lyme Regis that the Cobb was built on the remains of the ridge that originally protected the town. It is an attractive theory and helpfully explains whey the Cobb, the port of Lyme Regis is a mile from the ancient town. From then until now the history of the Cobb has been one of constant repair in the face of constant attack by the sea.

In Weymouth the first reference to land reclamation comes in 1242 when Anselm Capellanus paid a rent of 4d for a piece of land, 'won from the sea in the port of Weymouth' (pro quadam placia conquesta de mari in portu de Waymue), exactly where this piece of land was is unknown. Similarly in 1548 it was recorded that there was a charitable bequest of:

> xs xid [10 shillings 11 pence] yerelie hath been paid out of certeyn lands wthin the parishe of Sanwyche [Swanage] in the said Countie to the mayntenennce of See bankes there

And again there is no indication of where the 'See bankes' were.

It was during the seventeenth century that the technology finally became available to drain large areas of land. Hoping to take advantage of this technology it was in the spring of 1630 a group of gentlemen came together, probably at Abbotsbury, to plan something spectacular, the draining of the Fleet Lagoon, thirteen kilometres long stretching from Abbotsbury to Smallmouth near Portland and separated from the open sea by the shingle ridge of Chesil Beach. This was, perhaps, the most audacious civil engineering project to be carried out in Dorset in the seventeenth century, and indeed, was hardly to be surpassed until the coming of the railways.

The agreement for the draining of the Fleet was signed on 1 July 1630, in which the adventurers, to give them their seventeenth century title, agreed;

> To use their best skill and endeavours to and at ….. their own proper costs to drain a certain Mere Fleet or parcel of Saltmarsh being the inheritance of the said Sir John Strangways which, time whereof the memory of man is not to the contrary hath lain under water and over and upon which Mere or Fleets the sea doth and hath used to ebb or flow, commonly called or known by the name or names of East and West Fleets lying and being in the parishes villages limits or precincts of Abbotsbury Wyke Chickerell Fleet and Langton.

Sir John Strangways, the owner of the Abbotsbury Estate, was not, wisely as it turned out, investing any of his money in the scheme. He was supplying the land to be drained, and would receive;

> that part of the said Mere Fleet which is called or known by the name of the West Fleet heretofore severed or parted from the rest of the said Mere Fleet or Saltmarsh called the East Fleet by an ancient bank, ridge or causeway called Bridgehill on the east side thereof.

Work seems to have started at the beginning of 1631. The adventurers seem to have considered that Chesil Beach would provide a natural sea defence to the south west, a mistake that was to cost them dear, and so:

> They did bestow a very great deal of labour and charge in and towards the making of a great Dam or Bay of great breadth and length crossing between the land and the Sea Bank or Beach therein so much that to their very great charge and with much pain or labour the flowing of the broad Sea were restrained or stopped out by the said Dam or Barr from flowing into the said Fleet.

The dam was built of earth and rubble, and contained several sluice gates which seemed to have caused problems from the very beginning:

> About Mich'mas last one of the Sluices which stood in the great Bay was worn through by the violence of the Water which would have endangered the whole Work if it had not been speedily prevented. And also the walls of the great stone Sluice sunk and fell down insomuch as if it had not been remedied with speed it would as this Defendant believes have endangered the whole Work.

After the dam had closed the end of the Fleet pumps, powered by wind or water mills, were erected to pump the water away. As the water level dropped, drains were dug so that water from the streams that entered the Fleet at Abbotsbury, Langton Herring and elsewhere, could be led away safely. Apparently they had succeeded, as it was reported that, 'some part of the said Fleet was put in so good a way of Draining as that a man with boards fastened to his feet have gone thereupon', but then something went very wrong.

There was a difficulty which they had not foreseen. The lease had been drawn up on the understanding that Sir John Strangways owned the bed of the Fleet, but did he? When news of the activity in Dorset reached London someone realised that Sir John's ownership of the Fleet bed was far from clear. If it had been a fresh water lake there would have been no problem, but the Fleet was salt (or at least brackish) so was it an arm of the sea? If this was the case then it would belong to the Crown. A courtier, George Kirke, saw an opportunity. He collected evidence that the Fleet was an arm of the sea (and hence Crown Land), then sought and obtained:

> A grant of these premises … unto George Kirke one of his Majesty's Bed Chamber and Thomas Allen.

He seems to have been led to believe that the Fleet had already been drained and that he would receive, either several thousand acres of newly reclaimed land, or a payment from those who had actually done the work so that they could keep the land they had drained. He was to be disappointed. Storms during the winter of 1631/2 had damaged the works and the Fleet was again underwater.

George Kirke was furious and, convinced that the works had been deliberately sabotaged by the adventurers so that he would receive nothing for his grant. He had some reason, as Sir George Horsey admitted:

> That he …. being informed that George Kirke Esquire one of the Grooms of his Ma'te Bedchamber had procured from his Majesty a Grant of the said Fleet and intended to out and dispossess this Defendant and his partners thereof and to take the benefit of their Industry labour and Charge [he] did say rather that it should … turn again to a Fish Poole.

However it was nature, rather than deliberate sabotage that had destroyed the work, as George Penny reported:

> The Sea at times of stormy winds and Tempests hath soken & flowen through the said gravely or sandy bank into the said Fleet again and cannot without great labour and continual charge bee kept out also about Mich'mas last one of the Sluices which stood in the great Bay was worn through by the violence of the Water which would have endangered the whole Work if it had not been speedily prevented. And also the walls of the great stone Sluice sunk and fell down insomuch as if it had not been remedied with speed it would as this Defendant believes have endangered the whole Work. And thereupon he this Defendant did to his great charge of almost Forty pounds cause the same great breach to bee amended and stopped up again and so it now continues.

But these works required constant repair and Sir George knew what would happen if the works weren't maintained. He prophesised that the Fleet:

will of itself ... soon return to his ancient Form if this Defendant and his
Partners doe but hold their hand off it.

With storm damage to the dam and water coming through Chesil Beach he was swiftly
proved correct and the Fleet flooded again. George Kirke was left with the options of either
abandoning the project or draining the Fleet himself. He decided on the latter, but again
the drainage scheme failed and he passed any rights he had in the Fleet back to Sir John
Strangways. As for the rent to the crown:

The rent of 10£ per annum is not to be paid until the major part [of the
Fleet] be drained which is not nor will ever be done.

The attempts of the 1630s clearly showed that it was virtually impossible to drain the
whole of the Fleet, but the idea of land reclamation refused to go away. Thirty years later
another attempt was made, this time to drain a very small portion of the Fleet. In 1665
William Fry, steward of the Abbotsbury estate, obtained a lease to drain Herbury Ope.
Fry was a practical man who had chosen his ground well. The bay at Herbury is large and
shallow with a comparatively narrow entrance, (Ope is a local word for bay, still used on
Portland at Church Ope). His plan was simple, a sea wall was built across the entrance to
keep the waters of the Fleet out. The remains suggest that it was built of earth and rubble,
thirty metres wide, and fronted by a metre thick stone wall. A small stream flowed into the
bay from the north, but this would not have posed a problem to contemporary technology.
Similar sea walls, of seventeenth and eighteenth century date, can be found to the west of
Lymington in Hampshire. Though requiring regular maintenance, the design is an effective
one, and there seems to have been no reason why this scheme should have failed, but it did
so. Within a hundred and fifty years hardly anything was remembered of William Fry's
attempt. In 1808 Robert Pittman the decoyman at Abbotsbury, then aged 60, was asked
about past aspects of the Fleet. Amongst other things he:

Says that at a point called Yerbury in the Parish of Langton there is an
embankment thrown up called Frys works that it appears to be the remains
of an Old wall & has heard old people say that a man by the name of Fry
tried to drain that part of the Fleet. Don't know who Fry was.

The old sea wall at
Herbury.

In Weymouth the damage to the sea wall was due to human activity. By 1600 a substantial wall had been built to enclose the marshes to the west of the town. As usual these sea walls required constant care. For example the minutes of the town council record that on 14 October 1636:

> It is agreed that the Marsh belonging to this Borough shall be let out to such persons as will give most rent for the same, and that the walls and banks thereof shall be forthwith repaired and amended, and that such Tenant as shall rent the same shall covenant, to uphold the said walls and banks during his term, and at the end thereof to leave the same so sufficiently forthwith repaired and amended.

However politics took a hand and during the Civil War the walls were neglected, so when peace returned they urgently needed repair. The council minutes of 28 March 1651 record:

> That the Masons shall make up the old wall of the Marsh Four Foot high from the highest part of the foundation and so level all along, and of the same breadth that the wall was before and back it sufficiently with Clay, And shall make a bank level with the Top of the said wall six foot in breadth behind and adjoining to the wall besides the stone work of which six foot

Herbury from the air, the old sea wall is clearly visible.

they are to back sufficiently the stone work one foot and a half with blew clay, And they are to make the work and staunch, and to use good materials about it and to make it so as to keep out the water all materials to be provided at their charge save only such Tools as are in the Townes Custody fit for the work. They are to complete the work by the last of August next, and the Towne is to pay them Threescore pounds for the work.

A tide mill was place on the wall and was turned by water flowing through the wall into a pound behind it as the tide rose, then turned the other way as the tide fell and water drained away. In due course land was reclaimed in front of the wall, and the whole of the marsh disappeared under the developing town of Weymouth.

At Sandsfoot Castle, to the south of Weymouth erosion was threatening the castle. Here attempts were made to protect the castle. The castle had been built in 1540, but within a few years the outer defences of the castle were under threat. Between 1584 and 1586, repairs were undertaken to the castle which included

Filling up the great gulf which was wrought by the sea on the east side of the castle, and building a wall of ashlar upon the same, in height 22ft. and in length 60ft.

New making the vaults, being wholly decayed and sunk into the sea.

Twenty years later, during the two years 1610-11, yet more repair work was needed on the sea wall.

Pulling down a ruined wall, laying a foundation 60ft. long, 6ft. deep, and 10ft. thick, and rebuilding the old wall 15ft. above the foundations.

The carriage of " 400 tons of filling stuff " cost £20.

Making with ashlar stone the wall and parapet of a new platform and laying paving stones there.

A few years later, in 1623 yet more repairs were needed.

At the lower battery upon the water, one corner thereof the water hath undermined. The wall is of free stone very sufficiently built against the water towards the east and would be very convenient towards the west with a like wall 30 feet high, four and a half rods long (which makes nine rods of wall), 10ft. thick at the bottom and wrought with Portland stone, at £30 18s. 0d. a rod. This wall will prevent the undermining of this corner of the battery and " it were needful that it were looked unto in time " because the water daily undermines and eats away the ground. By estimation the cost of the wall is £278 2s. 0d.

Despite all these repairs the cliffs continued to be eroded by the sea, and by the 1660s the castle had been abandoned and began to fall into the sea. Whilst these defences failed, at Portland they were more successful. In 1623 it was reported that:

Also, towards the north-west side of the bridge the moat is daily overflowed by the sea, so that at high water there is no passage to the castle on that side; there, the moat must be mended with a counterscarp to withstand the sea and prevent its overflowing, which being 15 rods in length, at 45s. a rod, with

The successful sea
wall below Portland
Castle.

cleansing the moat, together with a stone traverse towards the sea to keep the
water in the moat and resist the force of the sea on that side, will amount to
£68 15s.

These repairs seem to have been much more effective, Portland Castle is still here, and
completely intact.

Apart from the development of the quays, and in the immediate vicinity of the towns
of Wareham and Poole, it was not until the seventeenth century that land drainage and
reclamation began to make a real impact on the landscape around Poole Harbour.

The meadows alongside the Frome below Wareham were drained during this period.
Writing in 1774 the historian John Hutchins claimed that:

> The tides formerly rose higher and the meadows on the north and south
> sides of the town were anciently morass, and covered by the water almost
> every tide, as they are even now on a spring tide, a south east wind and a
> flood. They have been improved and made firm ground by cutting drains, and
> raising the banks of the river, within the memory of man.

The narrow, enclosed, passage to Wareham.

In fact, during the sixteenth century the Frome estuary had been silting up, a problem that affected several ports along the southern cost of Britain at this time, and as a result there had been a massive decline in the port's trade. This draining was as much a means of keeping the port open, by ensuring all the water from the Frome ran down a single, comparatively narrow channel, as with creating additional pasture land. The idea of protecting the port failed, restricting the channel certainly meant that it would naturally be kept clear of silt, but by following the banks of the Frome the channel curved sinuously, meaning that only small vessels were able to reach Wareham. Interestingly, at the beginning of the nineteenth century, there were proposals to cut a canal linking Wareham to Poole Harbour. They were even shown on the chart of Poole Harbour drawn by Captain Sheringham in 1849, but instead the railway reached Wareham and these proposals came to nothing.

In 1673-4 more extensive proposals were made to reclaim land around the edge of the harbour:

> There seems formerly to have been a project, and a very unaccountable one, to embank, inclose, and recover these banks. It was found by inquisition, 13 Car. II. that the waste and oozy grounds in the bay, containing, by admeasurement, 8026 acres, and also *Gofts Bay* alias *Little Sea* bounded almost round with *Parkeston*, forty-one acres – *Holes Bay*, bounded on the E. by Parkston, with a neck of land called *Windmill Point*, and Pool on the E. Hamworthy or South Ham on the S. Upton-wood, Tottenham, and Hickord on W.N. and N.E. 885 acres- *S. Lichet Bay*, bounded by Hamworthy on the E. Holton on the W. and Licher on the N. 234 acres – *Sheepfall Bay*, bounded by Arne on the S.N. and W. 100 acres – *Middleburgh Bay*, bounded by Arne on the N.W. and Fitzoure on the S.E. which bay divides towards the W. into three creeks; one lying between Arne to the N.W. Middleburgh to the S. and Slepe on the S.W. – another between Middleburgh to the N. and Wych to the S. - another between Wych to the N. and Fritsoure to the S. 350 acres – *Sherwood Bay*, bounded by Fitzoure on the N.W. Owre on the S.W. sixteen acres - *Owere Bay*, lying between Owere on the W. and Newton to the S.E.

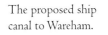
The proposed ship canal to Wareham.

eighty acres – *St. Andrews,* or *Browsey Bay,* bounded almost all round with Brownsey on the E.S and W. sixty eight acres – *Brand's Bay* lies between Newton to the W. and Studland and S. Haven Point to the E. and S.E. and lands called *Brands* to the S. 305 acres. These premises were granted to *Charles* duke of *Richmond* and *Lennox,* for thirty-one years, paying yearly 5 s. that within five years, he imbanked the premises at his own charge, and repaired and maintainded the banks, walls, and fences: a fourth part so imbanked, to be set out for the king. All or great part of the pre-miles were granted 17 Car. H. to *Charles Gifford,* esq, for forty-one years, paying yearly 6d. an acre, or a quarter of the yearly value of the lands so imbanked : but this project was found impracticable, and nothing was or could be done in it.

Although the enclosure and draining of these mudlands, 'was found impracticable,' it was not 'a very unaccountable one'. Though nothing happened at the time, nor indeed for the next fifty years as the unenclosed mud flats are clearly shown on the Map of Dorset by Isaac Taylor (1765), by the end of the century a great deal of drainage had taken place. The evidence for drainage in some of the areas mentioned is impressive, But, apart from two areas, the drainage appears to have been piecemeal, small plots, little more than individual fields, being drained rather than a very large area being drained in one big scheme.

The large areas, recognisable by their long straight sea walls, are to be found at The Moors, Swineham Point and at Keysworth, all round the western end of the Wareham Chanel. Swineham Point was one of the many schemes around the harbour to have failed, as the sea wall seems to have been breached in the early twentieth century. The land reclamation scheme at Keysworth is particularly interesting. The sea wall that exists today is clearly part of a large scheme, however aerial photographs show internal banks which may be evidence for an earlier piecemeal scheme.

The piecemeal schemes, enclosing and draining individual fields or groups of fields can

Failed sea walls at Middlebere, Poole Harbour.

be found in many places around the harbour. They can be recognised by their irregular boundary, individual farmers building banks that followed existing channels or enclosing slightly higher or firmer patches of mud. As well as the numerous fields that are still in use today, there are about twenty examples of failed schemes, recognisable in aerial photographs, by the remains of banks running across the mud.

One of the strangest stories of land reclamation concerns St Andrew's Bay, which lies at the eastern end of Brownsea Island. This is probably the best known failed land reclamation scheme in the harbour as the intertidal mud enclosed by the ruined sea wall forms an important feeding ground for wildfowl. The story usually given, can be summed up as follows. The bay was enclosed by Colonel William Waugh between 1852 and 1856, when he carried out various works on the island. A late nineteenth century owner of Brownsea considered that:

> The most valuable improvement of all was the embankment and wall reclaiming St Andrew's bay from the sea. The magnitude of this undertaking may be imagined when one is told that hundreds of barges of clay were sunk in the deep parts and over a million and a quarter of bricks were used for the wall.

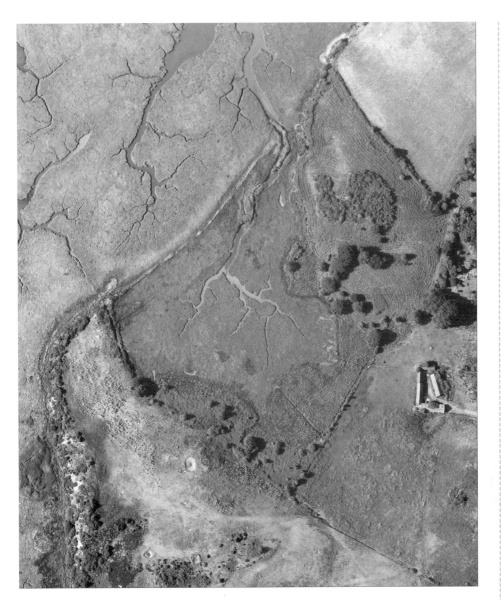

Failed sea walls at
Vitower, Poole
Harbour.

It is likely that this wall finally failed, owing to neglect, during the ownership of the island by Mrs Mary Bonham Christie between 1927 and 1939 when she allowed the island to 'return to nature'. However this is not the whole story. A chart of the harbour by Captain Sherringham, drawn in 1849, and a plan of the island drawn in 1853 both show a failed scheme, with broken banks enclosing an area of mud. The chart of Murdoch Mackenzie (1785) also shows the banks, on the same line but with slightly different breaks, which would not be unexpected considering that there is sixty years between the surveys.

Hutchins, quoted above, lists, 'St Andrews, or Browsey Bay, bounded almost all round with Brownsey on the E.S and W.', as one of the areas which it was considered desirable to drain. It would therefore seem that St Andrew's Bay was drained in the early to mid eighteenth century, but the sea walls failed and the reclaimed land reverted to saltmarsh for eighty or more years, so here we have the curious case of land being reclaimed then lost to the sea, not once but twice.

In the nineteenth century a substantial area of land was reclaimed at Poole which had the unusual effect of moving a place name:

The failed sea
defences at St
Andrew's Bay shown
on a chart of 1785.

Failed sea walls at
Swineham Point,
Poole Harbour.

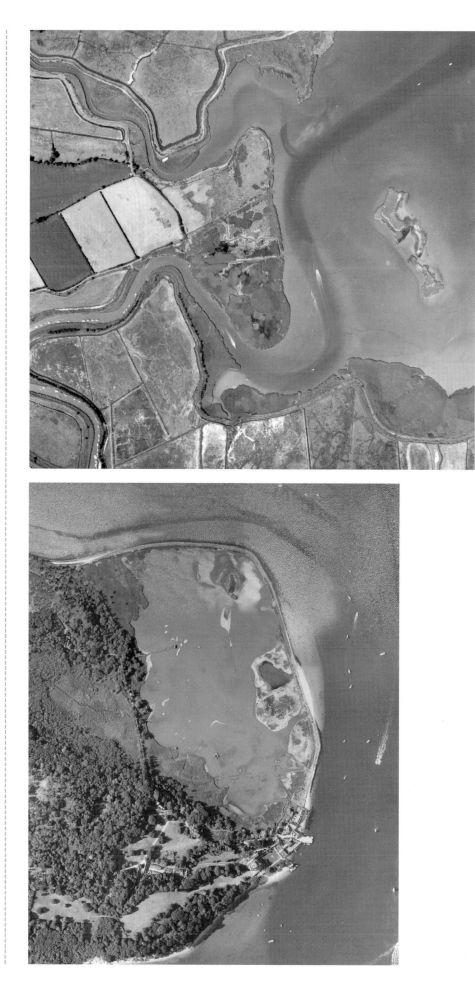

The failed sea
defences at St
Andrew's Bay on an
aerial photograph of
2005.

> In 1722, *Robert Dore* of *Limmington* was presented at a court of admiralty, for
> inclosing several acres of muddy ground, or flats, belonging to the harbour,
> at the E. part of Holes Bay, for which he had a grant from Sir J. Webb.

Though it was not for another hundred and fifty years that Holes Bay was drained. At this
time Holes Bay was the name given to the bay which lay to the east of the town, the bay to
the north west of Poole was then known as Longfleet Bay. This bay was partly enclosed
to the south west by the narrow peninsular of Baiter Point, which for centuries had been
regarded as a perfect location for structures that were best kept away from centres of
population. Hence during the eighteenth and nineteenth centuries it was the home to a
gibbet, gunpowder store and isolation hospital. Although there was some smaller
reclamation around the edges of the bay during the eighteenth century, reclamation only
started in earnest after the building of the railway from Poole to Bournemouth in 1874
which cut off a large section of the bay (this is now the boating lake in Poole Park) and
encouraged the draining of more land for building. However, it wasn't until the well into
the twentieth century that the rest of the bay was drained, and the name transferred to
Longfleet Bay (which is now forgotten). What was once the site of site of a gibbet and a
hospital for infectious diseases is now a popular residential part of Poole.

Evidence of a much smaller land reclamation scheme can be found at Fleet, just below
Moonfleet Manor Hotel, formerly Fleet Manor House. Here a small bay is closed off by
the remains of a sea wall and other walls link this to the coast. Other structures in the area
include the remains of a nineteenth century pier and a small artificial island, probably also
nineteenth century.

Apart from the pier nothing is recorded of these structures, though a local tradition,
calls the island "Gun Island" because it was said to be a stand for wildfowlers from Fleet
Manor. This is quite probably true and, apart from the pier, the other structures do not seem
to be explicable in purely functional terms. The Fleet is very shallow beyond the walls and
the land enclosed is hardly sufficient to make the effort of draining it for agricultural
purposes worthwhile. If not functional, could they have an aesthetic function? might they

Baiter Point, Poole
in 2005, a desirable
place to live.

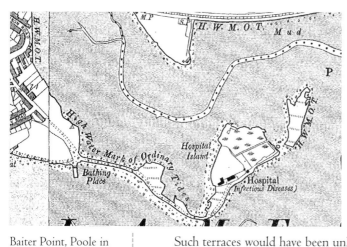

Baiter Point, Poole in 1886, a place for infectious diseases.

The earthworks in the Fleet by Moonfleet Manor Hotel.

'Gun Island', where shooting parties would congregate.

be early garden features, associated with Fleet Manor House?

Fleet Manor House was first built in the mid seventeenth century, enlarged over the centuries, and by the mid eighteenth century, was surrounded by formal gardens. Unfortunately the surviving views of the house do not include the Fleet shore. It is possible that the walls were built at this time, creating a formal terrace along the shore of the Fleet. This would be in keeping with the early eighteenth century style of garden, which delighted in rigid formality.

Such terraces would have been unlikely to survive the year 1824 when a violent storm devastated this part of Dorset, and virtually destroyed the neighbouring village of Fleet. It is known that the grounds of Fleet Manor were extensively refurbished in the late 1820s and it is likely that, at this time, Gun Island was constructed of the tumbled remains of the walls.

As far as is known this is the first time that garden features have been identified in an intertidal or maritime context.

At Highcliffe it was an attempt to save the garden which led to the first coast defences there. The cliffs here are very soft and have been actively eroding for centuries, in some years several metres of the coast can fall into the sea. In the early nineteenth century the first High Cliff House (precursor of Highcliffe Castle) was built so close to the edge of the cliff that it was in constant danger of destruction from landslips. Within ten years of the building of the house there were only sixty feet between the mansion and the cliff and it is said that the old gardener used to try to hide fresh havoc by turfing over the scene of each new fall of earth. The original builder of the house, Lord Bute loved the house but his grandson who inherited the property was less enamoured. There were clearly attempts made at the time to shore up the cliffs and prevent or slow down the rate of erosion, however these all failed. After a few years Charles Stuart sold the property, realising that here he could never win against the tide, the new owner demolished the house and rebuilt it a few hundred yards inland guessing, correctly as it turned out, that it would be many years before erosion threatened the new property.

At Hengistbury Head the situation was very different, here the coast had natural protection in the form of large ironstone boulders which lay along the bottom of the cliff. In the early 1840s, John Holloway, a local coal merchant, began to bring coal into Christchurch by sea. At first his boats returned empty to Southampton, but this wasn't profitable and he was soon looking for a return cargo. He found it in the ironstone which outcropped on Hengistbury Head, and a company, Hengistbury Mining Company was established in order to quarry on the head. By 1849, instead of only quarrying he was also removing the ironstone boulders that lined the seaward shore of the head. Within a few years the removal of this natural defence was making itself felt and the head was eroding. A long spit of sand formed, almost blocking the entrance to the harbour. Despite many protests quarrying continued until 1870, and the head has been under threat from erosion ever since. The Hengistbury Mining Company was probably the most expensive mistake ever made on the Dorset coast.

This almost suicidal madness was to be found elsewhere on the coast, at the other end of the county in Lyme Regis, which had spent so much energy in protecting its port with the building and constant maintenance of the Cobb:

> The erosion at Lyme has been accelerated by human agency, for while the townsfolk were engaged in ceaseless warfare against the sea their best defence against it was being removed and shipped to London to supply material for the erection of stucco houses. Thousands of tons of limestone were being quarried from the ledges of rock on the foreshore before the town in the early nineteenth century. The quarrying for lime of both reefs and cliffs continued here until recently [written in 1921], thus accelerating the recession of the coast both directly and indirectly through the resultant deepening of the water in front of the town.

Until the 1970s gravel was being dug from Chesil Beach, before it was finally accepted that what geologists had been saying for nearly a century, that Chesil Beach was not receiving any new gravel, was true and removing the shingle was putting the coast of West Dorset in greater danger.

From the mid nineteenth century onwards people became more concerned with stopping or slowing coastal erosion. This was commonly done by erecting groynes running down the coast. These can be effective, as they work by preventing the sea moving shingle along the beach. Thus shingle will build up on one side of the groyne but be swept clear on the

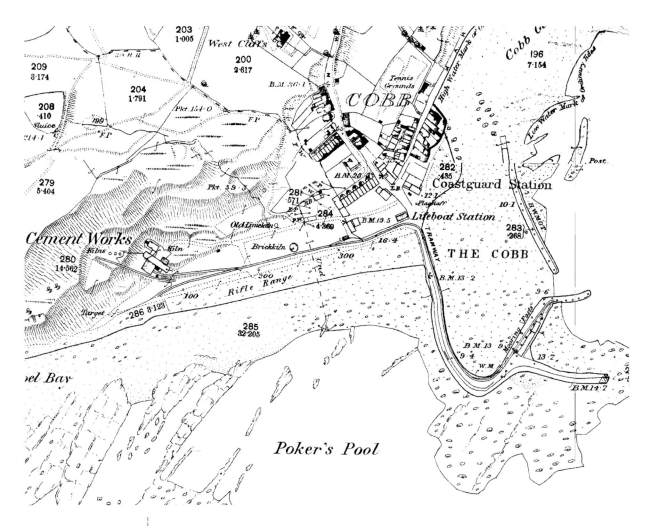

The cement factory at Lyme Regis.

other. This effect can clearly be seen at West Bay. When the eighteenth century harbour was built the first piers were open timber structures through which shingle could pass. On the chart drawn by Lt. Mackenzie in 1787, nearly fifty years after the piers were built the shingle on either side of the harbour mouth is at the same level. In 1823-4 the piers were rebuilt as solid structures. Over the next hundred years the shingle built up on the eastern side of the pier, whilst to west the shingle disappeared and the coast eroded. Now at West Bay there is a large beach on the eastern side, and expensive coastal defence works on the west!

As well as affecting erosion at other places along the coast, sea defences need constant work to repair and replace. If defences are abandoned then the sea will commonly overwhelm them fairly quickly. A few years ago the stumps of ancient timbers were found projecting from the beach in Ringstead Bay. The finder reported this, thinking it was an ancient shipwreck buried in the beach. When a marine archaeologist came to investigate this find he was puzzled at first, until he noticed two more wooden stumps which formed a straight line with the first. Careful probing in the beach revealed other stumps – it was all that was left of an early twentieth century groyne!

People's attitude to sea defences is always altering. Now there is a movement which believes in the removal of 'hard defences' and allowing nature to take it course. This is known as 'Managed Retreat', and it is hoped that this will delay coastal erosion in some places. On the other hand at Boscombe a new 'high tec' approach is being trialled, the Boscombe surf reef. This consists of a bank of sandbags placed offshore aimed at creating an area for high quality surfing. As well as a recreational site this is also intended to act as a sea defence because, according to the council's publicity:

Reefs decrease the rate of erosion on beaches by dissipating wave energy before it has a chance to hit the beach.

And they are better than other forms of coastal defence because:

Reefs are submerged offshore structures, supporting the natural beauty of the beach and ocean, unlike prominent seawalls or groyne structures, which can be unsightly and create blight.

Though whether that will work as intended is yet to be determined. All that can be said is that the coast will continue to erode, as it as done in Dorset for the past twelve thousand years, and people will continue to be affected by it and try to control it as they have done for millennia.

Bridport Harbour in 2005, erosion is now a problem on the western side of the pier.

6: Enjoying the Sea

TOURISM IS SUCH A PART OF THE DORSET COAST, and visitors are so important to the area's economy, that it is difficult to appreciate that this has not always been the case, and that there was a time when visitors were looked upon with suspicion, as potential criminals, traitors and spies.

On 11 October, 1636 the town council of Weymouth and Melcombe Regis:

> Agreed that wheras many abuses have been comitted by the Pilotts of this Borough in bringing in strangers that come into this Harbour unto Inns and private Howses without making Mr. Mayor or any officer of this Towne acquainted therwth, by meanes whereof many abuses have been and are dayly comitted wch escape unpunished, and many a dangerous and suspitous person departs unexaied [unexamined] It be ordered: That for the future noe Pilott allowed by the Towne shall bring any person on shore out of any ship that shall come into this Harbour or roade [anchorage] (of what quality soever) but he shall first bring such partys unto the Mayor for the tyme being, or in his absence unto the then Baylives, that notice may be taken, what he is, whence he came, whither bound, and such other questions demanded of him as shall be then be thought fitt, and the quality of the person shall require, upon payne that each pylott offending herein shall upon the offence proved or confessed before Mr. Mayor be turned out of his office, and another chosen in his steed.

Seventy years later, the attitude of the authorities in Weymouth remained the same. On 26 July 26, 1705 the writer Daniel Defoe, a political pamphleteer as well as a novelist, was arrested as a 'dangerous and suspitous person'. The Mayor, as the local magistrate, took him to Dorchester where the judges were then sitting, according to Defoe, in a pamphlet he wrote at the time:

> The Impertinence being discovered, the Mayor was sent back, the Gentlemen Dismiss'd, and the Wise Magistrate thought it his Duty to send up a letter to the Court to inform her Majesty's Secretaries of State what an Officious B was trusted with the Government of that Corporation.

And he advised his readers;

> Let him not come near the Town of *Weymouth*, in Dorsetshire, lest the
> Worshipful Mr. Mayor cry out, *A Presbyterian Plot* : and not daring to meddle
> with him Personally shall put all his Hearsays, Supposes, and Druncken
> Evidences together and carry all the Honest People he can find that Converse
> with to *Dorchester* before a Judge, where accusing the Peace-maker of a
> Phanatick Plot, and a Bloody Design to perswade Folks to a Peaceable
> Rebellion, he comes Home with a Flea in his Ear, much about as wise as he
> went.

However the situation was soon to change. Travel became easier and safer, but there still had
to be a reason for travel, and the spas supplied it: you travelled for your health. By the mid
eighteenth century the inland spas were very popular. The first to develop had been those
near London such as Epsom and Tunbridge Wells, later ones further afield the most
important of which was Bath.

Then in the year 1753, Dr Charles Russell, an English doctor, published the book *The
Uses of Sea Water*, advocating sea bathing and even drinking sea water as a way of promoting
good health. Within a few years coastal towns had begun to develop as holiday resorts, and
they never looked back.

The story of Dorset's coastal resorts has been told in many place and on many
occasions, and will not be repeated here, rather the ways in which the resorts made use of
the sea in their development, through bathing, sailing or, in the remarkable story of Lyme
Regis, the effects of coastal erosion.

WEYMOUTH

Weymouth was the first true seaside resort in Dorset, and one of the earliest in the country.
In 1750 Ralph Allen first visited the town. He was a remarkable man who had made a
fortune through reorganising the Post Office, and the development of Bath as a fashionable
spa. It seems that his wife was ill and, the waters of his home city not working their cure,
she had been advised to try sea bathing and drinking sea water. This seemed to work, so

The 'Old Rooms'
Weymouth's first
Assembly Room,
built in 1760. It was
the building that
began the
development of
Weymouth as a
holiday resort.

much so that for the next few years the Allens visited the town every summer. Over the next few years other fashionable people followed them, including the Duke of Gloucester, the king's younger brother, who built Gloucester Lodge overlooking Weymouth Bay in 1757.

In November 1788, King George III was taken ill and a course of sea bathing was prescribed. The Duke of Gloucester soon offered his Weymouth house to his ailing brother for the following summer. So, on 30 June 1789, at four in the afternoon, the Royal Party arrived. They were met with all due pomp and ceremony, there was a band playing 'God save the King' and with gun salutes from both the Nothe battery and Portland Castle.

Weymouth seafront from the Cyclorama, with an early paddle steamer entering the harbour. The long curve of the esplanade, 'the pride of Weymouth', is clearly shown.

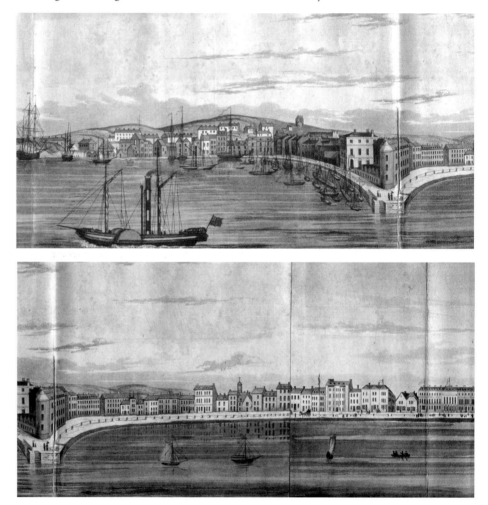

There is a wonderful first hand account of George's first visit to Weymouth, in the diaries of Fanny Burney, one of the ladies of the court:

Gloucester House, which we now inhabit, is situated in front of the sea, and the sands of the bay before it are perfectly smooth and soft. . . . The bay is very beautiful after its kind ; a peninsular shuts out Portland Island and the broad ocean.

The bathing machines make it their motto over all their windows, and those bathers that belong to the Royal dippers wear it in bandeaux on their bonnets to go into the sea, and have it again in large letters round their waists to encounter the waves. Flannel dresses tucked up, and no shoes nor stockings, with bandeaux and girdles have a most singular appearance, and when first I surveyed these loyal nymphs, it·was with some difficulty I kept my features in order.

Nor is this all. Think but of the surprise of his Majesty when, the first time of his bathing, he had no sooner popped his Royal head under water than a band of music, concealed in a neighbouring machine, struck up 'God save great George our King.'

The Magnificent, a man-of-war of 74 guns, is now stationed at the entrance of the bay for the security and pleasure of the King; and a fine frigate, the Southampton, Captain Douglas, is nearer in, and brought for the King to cruise about.

Almost miraculously, the king's health began to improve. He enjoyed his sea bathing and his riding excursions along the coast and trips out to sea in the 32-gun frigate Southampton. So began a happy (and economically rewarding!) sixteen year association between King George and the little towns of Weymouth and Melcombe Regis. The royal family made a total of fourteen visits between 1789 and 1805.

During this time Weymouth became the pre-eminent seaside resort in the country, people came to the town to bathe, sail and, of course to see the Royal Family in a remarkably informal setting. In 1804 one of these visitors was Cassandra Austen, Jane Austen's elder sister. She was disappointed in her visit to the town, which was commented on in typical caustic fashion by her younger sister.

I take the first sheet of this fine striped paper to thank you for your letter from Weymouth, and express my hopes of your being at Ibthrop before this time. I expect to hear that you reached it yesterday evening, being able to get as far as Blandford on Wednesday. Your account of Weymouth contains nothing which strikes me so forcibly as there being no ice in the town. For every other vexation I was in some measure prepared, and particularly for your disappointment in not seeing the Royal Family go on board on Tuesday, having already heard from Mr. Crawford that he had seen you in the very act of being too late, but for there being no ice what could prepare me? Weymouth is altogether a shocking place, I perceive, without recommendation of any kind, & worthy only of being frequented by the inhabitants of Gloucester. I am really very glad that we did not go there, & that Henry & Eliza saw nothing in it to make them feel differently. Friday Sept 14. 1804 - Jane Austen

Though there could be worse things than a lack of ice at Weymouth.

The morning being remarkable calm and serene , induced the bathers, one and all, to enjoy themselves in the water; at half past twelve, the attention of the people, who were walking up and down the sands, was particularly taken up with a number of porpoises, scudding into the bay at an amazing rate, making the water fly before them like a violent spray, the fishermen all pronounced this a very extraordinary matter and such as they had never beheld before;: - upon further inspection with their glasses they plainly perceived that the porpoises were chased by nine remarkably large sharks,; the porpoises were making the best of their way to the shoal water among the bathing machines, the sharks closely pursuing them, which put the bathers into the utmost fright and confusion, so that it was with the utmost difficulty that the machines could be drawn from the water, without running foul of each other; one machine, however was unluckily overset, but fortunately no

This late eighteenth
century view of
Weymouth not only
shows the curving
bay, but also the early
pleasure craft, such as
the rowing barge in
the foreground.

other mischief happened, except one of the bathers being frightened into
convulsions, … However the porpoises, taking a coastwise direction along
the shore, among the rocks and shoals, baffled every attempt of the sharks,
who all put about, and stood into Weymouth Bay again, where they remained
until sun-set, and then stood out to sea on the ebb tide.

Happily events like this, which sounds like a scene from the film *Jaws*, have never happened
again at Weymouth, and bathing continued to be popular.

In the years following the end of the Napoleonic War the town continued to grow
steadily. It soon lost its reputation as a health resort:

The crowded beach
and esplanade
around the beginning
of the twentieth
century

What shall I say of Weymouth itself as a bathing-place ? Why, that had I
friends in perfect health, desirous of spending a couple of months during the
summer by the sea-side on the south coast, and at the same time indifferent
as to the particular spot they inhabited for that object, I would, on their

A similar view fifty years later, in the Golden Years of seaside tourism.

asking my advice, tell them by all means to spend them at Weymouth. But I should not say so to any patient, labouring no matter under what disease; for the situation of Weymouth is not fit for patients.

I happened to be travelling upon the Southampton Railway, as far as Andover, one day, in company with a gentleman who had been two years resident in Weymouth, and who praised much its pure and invigorating air, and the cheerful ensemble of the place; " but," said he, " my rheumatism won't stand any longer the dreadful east winds, and my poor daughters cough worse than ever since we settled there, and so we are about to leave it at the suggestion of my doctor, whom I had just been to town to consult."

But it continued to grow as a suitable base for bathing and sailing. This was helped in the 1850s when the railway reached the town in 1857, and the first of the tourist paddle steamers began to operate from the harbour.

The London and South Western Railway and the Great Western Railway line from Bristol met at Dorchester, and jointly operated the line to Weymouth. This meant that Weymouth was placed in the enviable position of being just three hours from London, two hours from Bristol and (when the Severn Tunnel was opened in 1886) just three hours from the heavily populated mining towns of South Wales. Now middle class families and factory workers could afford summer seaside holidays for the very first time.

The Paddle Steamers were soon a feature of the coast, the firm of Cosens, based in Weymouth, soon dominated the local trade and were always looking for opportunities to

At Weymouth bathing has always been an important part of the holiday experience. Two daring ladies take to the water in about 1920.

attract more and more visitors to use their boats. This began as early as 1859 when special boat trips were laid on to take visitors to look over Brunel's super-ship the Great Eastern as she lay in Weymouth Bay undergoing repairs after an accident on her maiden voyage.

This blend of bathing and sailing served Weymouth well for the next century and it was not until the development of cheap package holidays in the latter half of the twentieth century, that the resort's popularity began to decline. However, even today, sailing is still an integral part of Weymouth's appeal, and in 2012 Weymouth Bay will be hosting the sailing events of the London Olympics.

LYME REGIS

If the sea brought Weymouth prosperity through bathing and sailing, then Lyme Regis rose to prominence through a generally destructive aspect of living by the sea, coastal erosion. The soft lias cliffs of Lyme Regis are constantly eroding, and contain some of the most amazing fossils to be found in Britain.

The early history of Lyme tourism mirrored that of Weymouth, though in a less grand manner. This was outlined by George Roberts in 1834, in the earliest proper history of Lyme Regis:

During the summer months a few invalids occasionally came to enjoy the sea-air; but as machines were unknown, any one wishing to court the embraces of Neptune was obliged to undress on the beach: the accommodations in other respects were equally bad. Till after the construction of the turnpike road from Charmouth through Lyme to Exeter, in 1758, strangers in their journey westward had no opportunity of viewing it. The innkeeper first procured a bathing-machine for the accommodation of travellers, who were enabled to take a dip in a comfortable manner, before proceeding on their journey. It is a curious fact that he placed it at the mouth of the river, where it remained for several years. Bathing soon became a favourite, or rather fashionable prescription, with medical practitioners. Many a lovely creature, whose tender frame was shaken by an insidious malady beyond hope of cure, shivered at each plunge; and those in robust health were daily seen in numbers playing mermaids and tritons. Nearly every visitor of the coast was a bather.

Housekeepers near the sea began to fit up two or three front rooms in a homely manner, they met with encouragement, others were procured, and it soon happened, as it is somewhere expressed, that the invalids who came in search of health " found the goddess propitious to their prayers, and returning to pay their vows, brought beauty and elegance in their train." An agreeable society was formed in the summer months. Some families professed themselves partial to Lyme; and a few gentlemen, animated by public spirit, caused the Assembly-rooms to be erected, which, conducted on the most liberal plan of-any in England, may be considered to have rescued the town from impending ruin.

Families of good fortune regularly came for the season, and many of the first visitors built houses near the sea, in spots which till then had been entirely neglected. In the course of a few years great changes took place.

At this time Lyme Regis was seen as a cheap alternative to Weymouth, and it was probably for this reason that Jane Austen's family came here in 1804. However Lyme Regis had a unique asset, its geology, and from the 1820s, when she discovered the first plesiosaur fossil (it was so amazing that the great French anatomist Georges Cuvier first thought that it was a fake!) – Mary Anning.

Mary Anning was not the first professional fossil collector associated with Lyme Regis. In the 1750s travellers on the coast road through Charmouth were offered fossils, curiosities, for sale by a Mr Lock known as the 'Cury-man' or 'Captain Cury'. This casual trade continued well into the nineteenth century, much to the irritation of one traveller.

Here we were assailed with hawkers of fossilized ammonites and echinites and pentacrinites, and many other stony-ites, all imbedded in marl or lias-slate, which are offered to the [passengers] of every public or private vehicle that halts to change horses at Charmouth, as oranges are tendered to the stagers who start from Hatchett's or the Gloucester [coaching inns]. The trade is a thriving one, and as organic remains are abundant in the lias formation at Lyme and its vicinity, particularly of the Saurian animals, it will never fail.

A few years later:

Mr. John Crookshanks, was the first collector of *curiosities* at Lyme. These were then called *curosities*. He went upon the shore in search of them, with a long pole like a gardenhoe, and had found many vertebrae, called here *verier berries*, and *fragments of jaws*, &c. This person resigned his business for a consideration of a yearly stipend to be paid. This being discontinued, he committed suicide, by jumping off the gun-cliff wall into the sea, in 1802. Richard Anning [Mary Anning's father] used occasionally to accompany Mr. Crookshanks. The fragments of fossils they found were considered to be, and so named, *bones of crocodiles' backs and jaws, ladies' fingers, John Dories, salmon*, &c.

In 1805 Richard Anning probably played host to a Swiss Geologist, Jean André Duc Luc.

He described what was probably the Anning's home:

> I made the acquaintance here, with one of the inhabitants' who knows the coast very well, because he visits it, from time to time, in search of fossils which he sells to strangers who resort here. At his house I saw some fine cornu Ammonis [Ammonites], and various other marine fossils.

Much has been written about Mary Anning, in recent years she has been depicted in so many different ways, from the amazingly talented child (beloved of writers for children for more than a hundred years) to a proto-feminist. In fact no one seems to know what to make of her and haven't since she was in her early teens.

Her father had been a carpenter who as a sideline collected fossils from the adjacent cliffs to sell to visitors. Mary, it seems, took to fossil hunting at an early age and sold her first fossil ammonite to a visiting lady when she was a small girl. After the death of her father fossil hunting became a way of supplementing her family's small income. At the age of 12 she helped her brother with the discovery of the first ichthyosaur to be scientifically described. From then on she worked as a professional fossil hunter, and made a number of very important discoveries, the first plesiosaur, pterodactyl and the first records of a number of fossil fish.

Nineteenth century drawings of the ichthyosaur & plesiosaur discovered by Mary Anning

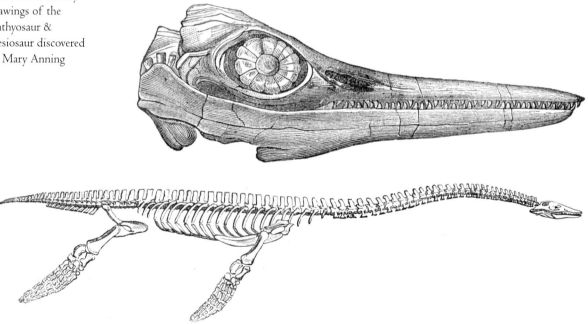

Her occupation, professional fossil hunter or 'fossilist', was unusual but not unknown at the time and she was undoubtedly one of the best and is certainly the best known – who now remembers Andrew Dupont, Anthony Merry and Mr Humphrey for example, who were also collecting at the time.

Much is now made about her supposed lack of recognition by the geological 'establishment' of the time, usually put down to prejudice, the male university educated geologists refusing to recognise the brilliance of a lower class woman. In fact the situation was rather different, she was more highly regarded than any other professional collector of the day, and her contributions to geological science were acknowledged. Her contemporaries recognised her as remarkable and treated her accordingly.

Also it must be remembered that, at this time, all the natural sciences were struggling for recognition as serious topics for study. Many people regarded them as idle pastimes, a

The Dorset sea with ichthyosaur and plesiosaur, as imagined in 1872.

gentleman might hunt for fossils as an alternative to fox hunting, though the latter was considered a more important activity! For example Joseph Pentland made detailed studies of ichthyosaur and plesiosaur skeletons in the 1820s, but refused to let his ideas be published under his name as his family did not consider geology a suitable subject for a gentleman to study. Palaeontology needed to be seen as a serious subject for study by learned men in learned societies, only then could the science progress.

Mary Anning didn't fit this scenario; even when she was working legends collected around her. The facts of her early life helped, the ordinary people of Lyme Regis knowing why she was so unusual: as a baby she had survived being struck by lightning!

> Mary was taken by her nurse, Aug. 19, 1800, to the Rack field [just inland from Lyme Regis], where some equestrians were to perform. In consequence of an extraordinary display of vaulting on the preceding evening, the spectators were very numerous. The weather was intensely hot and sultry ; the clouds seemed to indicate the approach of a thunder-storm, but did not deter the multitude from staying to witness the conclusion of the performance. At about a quarter to five P.M., a passing cloud discharged a heavy shower, which caused those assembled to effect a hasty retreat. Many betook themselves to the adjoining linhays [cattle sheds]; others went home; but the less prudent sought shelter under cover of some lofty elms that stood in the field. A vivid discharge of the electric fluid shortly ensued, followed by the most awful clap of thunder that any present ever remembered to have heard. All appeared deafened by the crash: after a momentary pause, a man gave the alarm, by pointing to a group that lay motionless under a tree. Some persons instantly ran to the spot, where there appeared three women and a child lying on the ground. All the grown persons were dead : the infant, Mary Anning, upon being put into warm water, revived : she had sustained no injury. She had been a dull child before, but after this accident became lively and intelligent, and grew up so.

Perhaps the best summation of the remarkable, 'handmaid of the geological sciences', as George Roberts her friend and historian of Lyme Regis called her, is to be found in the verses of another acquaintance, John Kenyon. These were written and published in 1838, during her lifetime.

To Mary Anning:

Thee, Mary! first 'twas lightning struck,
And then a water-vat half drowned
But I can't think 'twas mere blind luck
Twice left for dead-twice brought thee round
No! Fortune in her prescient mood,
I must believe, e'en then was planning
To fabricate a something good
Of Thee, the twice-saved Mary Anning.

This to fulfil she did not bid
Thy feet o'er foreign soils to roam,
For well she knew what powers lay hid
In these blue cliffs that touched thy home.
And hither led, in vain to Thee
Of marle, or rock, was insight banning;
Some folk can through a millstone see;
And so, in sooth, can Mary Anning.

Mere child as yet, this sea-beat strand
'Twas thine to wander all alone,
Upgathering in thy little hand
Chance-pebble bright, or fossil bone.
Though keenest winds were whistling round,
Though hottest suns thy cheek were tanning,
Nor suns, nor winds could check or bound
The duteous toils of Mary Anning.

At first these relic-shrouding rocks
Were but thy simple stock in trade,
Wherewith, through pain and worldly shocks,
A widowed mother's lot to aid.
But now, with taught and teaching eye,
Thy practised sense their sense is scanning;
And learning and philosophy
Both owe their debt to Mary Anning.

E'en poets shall by Thee set store;
For wonders feed the poet's wish;
And is their mermaid wondrous more
Than thy half-lizard and half-fish?
And therefore 'tis that, all the time
Yon shark's head Thou art measuring, spanning,
I inly weave this uncouth rhyme
In honest praise of Mary Anning.

True, Mary! We-earth-born-must go,
Like these lost tribes, to earth again,
Whilst Lyme's dark-headed urchins grow,

Each in his turn, to grey-haired men.
Yet when, grown old, this beach they walk,
Some pensive breeze their grey locks fanning,
Their sons shall love to hear them talk
Of many a feat of Mary Anning

This is the earliest reconstruction of a prehistoric environment. Originally a watercolour it was engraved as a handout for Professor William Buckland's geological students.

By the time Mary Anning died, in March 1847, the geology of Lyme Regis had become the unique feature of this sea side-resort. In fact as George Dunster said in his guide to Lyme Regis published in 1855:

> The death of Mary Anning, was a serious loss to the town, as her presence attracted a large number of distinguished visitors, who able to appreciate her genius, were desirous of perambulating with her, those shores which she had made celebrated : delighting to listen to her interesting descriptions, and instructive conversation.

Throughout the nineteenth century Lyme remained a quiet holiday resort, and although attempts were made to make it a fashionable destination, particularly after the arrival of the railway in 1903 it never really took off. Today the town still capitalises on its remarkable geology, even down to ammonites on the lampposts!

Lyme Regis still delights in its geological heritage.

SWANAGE

Swanage was a very late developer as a resort town. Although an ancient settlement it suffered from very poor communications with the rest of Dorset. Inland the main road to Corfe ran over the steep hill by Kingston, very difficult for any horse drawn vehicle. Access by sea was equally difficult as boats had to land on the beach. However around Swanage were small quarries producing some of the finest building stone in the country. For generations this had been exported by boats which were loaded directly from the cliffside quarries. Then in 1823 William Morton Pitt bought a substantial part of Swanage and developed the Manor House into a first class hotel. He added a pier and marine baths but, despite a

It was the pier that changed Swanage, although built for the stone trade, it allowed tourists to reach the town easily.

visit from the young Princess Victoria in 1833 (which led to the hotel being named the Royal Victoria Hotel) the town didn't really develop until the 1860s when the stone pier was built. This was intended to facilitate the export of stone, but it also meant that the popular paddle steamers could easily call at Swanage. For the next twenty years, until the railway came, most visitors arrived by steamer from Bournemouth or Weymouth.

As well as the visitors something else was arriving by ship, objects that would make Swanage unique and give it the nickname of 'Little London by the Sea'. George Burt, the leading stone merchant in Swanage was, at the time, sending a great deal of stone to London, mostly for paving the city's streets. His ships left Swanage heavily laden with stone,

Paddle steamers arriving at the new pier in Swanage at the beginning of the twentieth century.

but had no cargo for the return journey. However the ships needed something to ballast them, and George Burt had filled his yard with various objects removed from London streets during his development work. These now came to Swanage and during the latter part of the nineteenth century, bollards cast with the names of London parishes, various columns and even whole buildings or frontages of buildings. As a result the Town Hall, built in 1882, incorporates the front of the Mercers' Hall, from Cheapside, London, designed by Edward Jarman in 1668, whilst overlooking the bay is a tower, clearly missing its clock, originally built in 1854 at the southern approach to London Bridge, to commemorate the Duke of Wellington, and moved to Swanage in 1867-8.

As well as parts of old London, George Burt had new creations for Swanage. To the south of the town, on Durlston Head, he built Dorset's first theme park. This was intended to be the centrepiece of a new housing development, and whilst only a few of the houses were built, much of the park was. Landscaped paths led from Swanage, around the cliff edge to a mock castle, and the Great Globe. This is exactly what it says, a model of the earth, ten feet in diameter and weighing 40 tons, carved of Portland stone in 1887. It is surrounded by inscriptions giving useful information about the world and the universe. Similar texts are set in the walls along the paths, or short poems such as:

AN IRON COAST AND ANGRY WAVES,
YOU SEEM TO HEAR THEM RISE AND FALL,
AND ROAR ROCK THWARTED IN THEIR BELLOWING CAVES,
BENEATH THE WINDY WALL.
ABOVE SEA 149FT

Happily this amazing Victorian development survives and it now Durlston County Park, and freely available to all.

BOURNEMOUTH

Bournemouth is different to the other Dorset resorts in that it had no ancient origins. Lyme Regis, Weymouth and Swanage all had ancient forebears, but in 1800 Bourne Mouth was open heathland, only known as a gap in the cliffs and a landmark to local sailors.

The Great Globe at Durlston, part of George Burt's educational theme park.

In 1802 when the heathland was enclosed as a result of the Christchurch Inclosure Act, the principal local landowner, Sir George Tapps set about planting the area with pines. As yet there was no idea that the area could be developed as a resort. These pines did so well that one species, the Maritime pine, *Pinus pinaster*, gained an alternative common name of the Bournemouth pine.

In 1796 Louis Tregonwell, a Captain in the Dorset Yeomanry, had been made responsible for the defence of all the coastline between Christchurch and Poole Harbours. Tregonwell and his wife fell in love with the area. They bought 8 ½ acres of land and, by April 1812, they had built themselves a large house, now part of the Royal Exeter Hotel. Other houses soon followed built by Tregonwell and the principal landowner, Sir George Tapps-Gervis, son of Sir George. Bournemouth soon gained a reputation as a very healthy resort, and began to target the prosperous invalid.

> I would call your attention to the great capabilities of Bourne; for we look in vain elsewhere for that singular advantage which Bourne possesses, of presenting two banks of cliffs, clothed with verdure even at this inclement season, running from the sea inland, with a smiling vale watered by a rapid brook or bourne, dividing them just enough to allow of a most complete ventilation, with coolness in the summer months, and yet affording a most protected succession of ridges upon which to erect residences not only for convalescents, free from positive disease, but also for patients in the most delicate state of health as to lungs.
>
> For the latter the many glens which run up the western cliff, offer very beautiful retreats, surrounded by balsamic and almost medicinal emanations from fir plantations, which are found to be so beneficial in these cases.

Indeed by the middle of the century Bournemouth had:

> become celebrated all over the country as the best, the most promising, and the only real asylum for consumptive people of the higher order.

The investors in Bournemouth clearly saw that this would make their resort different from its neighbours. So care of the elderly and infirm dominated Bournemouth and was to do so for much of the century. An early guidebook described the town as being:

> as quiet and decorous as the most exacting could wish.

Whilst the other Dorset resorts welcomed the coming of the railway, Bournemouth was opposed to it at first.

> Tis well from far to hear the engines' scream.
> And see the distant, curling plume of steam,
> But let not Bournemouth – health's approved abode,
> Court the near presence of the iron road!

So went one anti-railway verse. The railway eventually did get to Bournemouth, in 1870 at the end of long, curving and inconvenient branch line. It wasn't until 1888 that the town was connected to the main line.

If railways were unpopular then boat trips were not. They were a good way of getting plenty of sea air, doubtless good for a recovering invalid.

Bournemouth was created as a health resort, and the pier has always been important.

As early as 1849 a regatta was held off the coast of Bournemouth, and in 1855 a wooden jetty was built on the beach close to the outlet of the stream, precursor of a pier, also of wood, that was to supersede it some years later.

Simultaneously with the planning of the town and the draining of its site, the laying out of the cliff and the approaches to it was proceeded with, and in 1859 the first piles of a wooden pier were driven in opposite the Bath Hotel in the presence of many invited guests. The work, however, had not proceeded far before a fierce gale swept everything away; but this misfortune did not check the enthusiasm of the Commissioners, who immediately began to build another pier which was completed in 1861. A grand fête was held to celebrate the opening, and for the next six years the pier entirely fulfilled the expectations of the most sanguine. Unfortunately, however, in the terrible storm of 1867 that wrought such havoc all along the southern coast, and was responsible for many wrecks, the whole of the seaward end of the pier, which was of the shape of a T, was torn up and flung with such force upon the beach as to be broken to pieces. What remained could still be used as a landing place from small boats but it too was seriously injured a year later, and it was decided not to attempt to repair it, but to replace it with an iron pier as soon as the necessary funds could be collected. Meanwhile, a temporary embarkation stage was erected, and it was from it in 1868 that the first steamboat excursion started from Bournemouth, when a Southampton vessel, the *Fawn*, took a party to Spithead to witness the Review of the Fleet in honour of the Shah of Persia, then on a visit to England. During the next ten years various enterprising companies competed with each other in running pleasure boats between Bournemouth and Weymouth or the Isle of Wight.

The present iron pier was begun in 1878, and opened by the Lord Mayor of London in 1880.

This is the pier that, substantially rebuilt, survives today.

Despite its rising popularity Bournemouth continued to cater for the elderly and infirm. As late as 1929 one visitor complained that:

> Fortunate indeed was the casual visitor who could obtain a morsel to eat on a Sunday anywhere except at one of the hotels which were open to non-residents. The tramways did not run and such harmless amusements as bands and sea bathing were ruled out entirely at Bournemouth on the Sabbath.
>
> In Bournemouth at many of the largest hotels, a request for a hot bath after 10p.m. is regarded by the management as most unreasonable to say the least of it. The invariable reply to such a rash proposition is that they are sorry but the chambermaids go off duty at 10 o'clock and are responsible for seeing that all bathrooms are locked up before they retire to bed. The free use of bathrooms should be available to visitors who desire them, paying as they do the highest rates for their bedrooms. Yet these bathrooms are as rigidly guarded and locked up as any strong room in the Bank of England.

Boscombe, a daughter settlement of Bournemouth. During the early twentieth century it was seen as more 'select' than Bournemouth.

Yet on the other hand Bournemouth was at the forefront of modern activities. An air display was held in Bournemouth as early as 1910, and houses were advertised as having garages for the new motor cars.

SPORT

Today if we talk about sport along the Dorset coast we think about yachting and rowing, or perhaps swimming and various beach sports. But two hundred years ago sport had a very different meaning. The chapter on sport in the *Victoria County History*, published in 1908 includes hunting, shooting, angling and horse racing, yachting isn't mentioned and apart from a very short description of sea fishing, no coastal or maritime sports are mentioned at all. The reason for this is simple, there were virtually no such sports practised at the time. This can be seen in the detailed accounts of the visits of George III and others to Weymouth in the late eighteenth and early nineteenth century, bathing and a little, rare, pleasure boating were the only maritime recreations that were generally practised.

WILDFOWLING

Considering the importance given to the protection of game, with very strict laws and regulations concerning what could be shot and who could shoot it, it is curious that very little attention was paid to wildfowl, as they were not regarded as the property of the landowner. So, as the indefatigable sportsman Colonel Peter Hawker remarked in 1830:

> Any one may shoot them on the coast, from a public path. Where a person, with neither permission from the lord of the manor nor license, has a right to carry a gun, provided he does not use it for the destruction of game.

What this mean was that wildfowl were free for anybody to shoot, as is evident from Peter Hawker's diaries, even though he didn't appreciate the presence of other, less skilled 'sportsmen'.

> January 13th 1813, — The wild fowl at last came into the haven [Poole] by thousands, in one continued succession of swarms, and in a few hours, an immense levy en masse of shooters was assembled at all points, and there was not a neck of land, bank, or standing place of any kind but what was crowded with blackguards of every description, firing at all distances, and completely annihilating the brilliant prospects of sport.
>
> January 14th. 1814 — It blew such a tremendous hurricane that comparatively few birds would fly, as they could remain unmolested in the harbour from the impossibility of the numerous host of boats and canoes being able to follow them. Some, however, came out and would have afforded charming sport, but after I had been at the trouble and expense of making proper masked entrenchments of every kind, I had in all quarters the mortification to find myself closely surrounded by vagabonds of every description, who were standing quite exposed, firing at seagulls, ox-birds, and even small birds, and repeatedly, as the geese were coming directly for me, like a pack of hounds full cry, I had to endure the provocation of seeing some dirty cabin boy spring up and drive them away with the paltry discharge of an old rusty popgun. Had it been possible for me to have lain peaceably in any one place, I should have filled a sack ; as it was, however, I had no further satisfaction than that of killing more than all these ruffians put together. I got 3 widgeon, 2 grey plover, 2 cormorants, 1 ring dotterel, 18 ox-birds, and

I dusky grebe. Had the coast been quiet, I should, of course, have only fired at proper wild fowl. When the rabble could not see to shoot they adjourned to the 'Haven' to drink, and when the liquor gave them fresh courage the guns were again taken out, and finding it too dark to see to fire at anything they began to amuse themselves with shooting in the air, till I was obliged to put a stop to it.

As well as shooting, another way of catching wildfowl was by means of a decoy. This was a complex structure, with a central pond from which a number of channels, called pipes, ran. The ducks were encouraged along these pipes which were encased in netting, to a cage at the end, where the wild ducks would be caught. There were once at least four decoys in Dorset, the most famous, and the only one that survives, is at Abbotsbury. This was originally built in 1655-6. In September 1917, Joseph Whitaker, the great expert on British Decoys visited Abbotsbury.

I went via Weymouth to see this decoy and swannery. When changing trains at Poole I thought of Colonel Hawker and the shooting he did there in those long past days. On arriving at Abbotsbury Station I found Mr. Hutchings, Lord Ilchester's agent, and was glad to be able to thank him for having so kindly given me information about the decoy. He now told me the keeper, Gill, would be at the decoy and ready to show it to me when I got there, which I did about 6 p.m. Down a short lane and over a meadow and I found the old decoyman waiting for me. He told me he had held the post for 38 years, and had been on the estate for over 50....... We now turned our attention to the decoy. There are four pipes, three of which open from the decoy pool, which is about 1 ¼ acres in extent, surrounded by 3 or 4 acres of reeds, and on one side by some storm-blown trees draped with lichen. The fourth pipe opens into the backwater, and this is the one in which the most ducks are taken. One day over 100 teal were secured. The most ducks ever got in a short time was a few years back when about 500 were captured in two days, 77 being caught at one take. A better situated decoy I have not seen, and the decoyman, I am sure, is an adept in decoying, and I much enjoyed my chat. It was getting dark and the sun was dipping westward before

The Abbotsbury swannery in the early twentieth century.

I could tear myself away from a spot which thoroughly appealed to my feelings, and I shall long remember the pleasant chat, the beautiful evening, and the quiet decoy so peacefully placed in that western county. Long may the swans float on the rippling waters, and may it be long, long years before the decoy is given up, as I am sorry to say so many have been in this our dear England.

A long forgotten aspect of this type of sport was falconry: birds were not killed on the coast, rather the cliffs were seen as a source of young falcons. There were even primitive conservation measures put in place.

The Dorset falconer is fortunate in living in a county which is still one of the greatest strongholds of our most noble British falcons, the peregrine (Falco peregrinus). Between St Alban's Head and Bridport there are still several eyries of these falcons, where annually, in spite of wanton destruction by guns and traps and the depredations of egg hunters, a fair number of young peregrines are bred each year.

From time to time the lover of bird life may recognize the graceful flight of these splendid falcons, as they sail high over the Dorset moors or open downs. For many years the writer used to employ men to watch and guard most eyries of peregrines along the Dorset cliffs. On occasions certain of the young birds, commonly called eyesses, would be taken from the nests for the purpose of training them, others being left and allowed to fly away. The local cliff climbers were paid a good price for all birds whether taken or not, in order to outbid the professional egg hunters who were always willing to pay a certain price for the eggs.

It was early in 1887 that the writer first commenced his attempts at falconry. Acting under the advice of an old friend, the late Major C. H. Fisher of Stroud in Gloucestershire, the greatest falconer of his day, he began by training two eyess peregrines taken from a nest near Lulworth Cove. Although he has owned innumerable falcons and hawks and flown them in many lands since those days, his earliest vicissitudes, pleasures and disappointments, pertaining to the first few seasons of a career as a falconer, will ever linger in his memory.

Now there is very little wildfowling in Dorset, bird watching having taken its place. The Fleet is managed as a nature reserve. Together with Poole Harbour it is protected for its rich bird life, and peregrine falcons still soar over the Dorset cliffs.

YACHTING

The idea of sailing for pleasure didn't really begin until the eighteenth century. People undoubtedly enjoyed travelling by sea before then, but the concept of doing it just for fun doesn't seem to have existed. It was expensive and therefore just for the wealthy, and it was just sailing, not racing, what we would now call cruising.

The development of yacht racing took place towards the end of the eighteenth century. In Dorset the development of the first racing yachts can be ascribed to the work of Joseph Weld of Lulworth. The Welds of Lulworth Castle were an old Roman Catholic family. In 1784 Thomas Weld decide to build a yacht, intended to sail gently from one port to another with groups of friends and families on board. Unfortunately the only person he could find to build his yacht was a man from Weymouth who set to work on the beach at Arish Mell with the estate carpenters, but who it was later found to have never built anything bigger than a rowing boat.

The project aroused great local interest, and crowds came from all the neighbouring parishes to admire the vessel. This was until the hull was more or less finished when it transpired that the designer had very little idea how to proceed with her masts and rigging, still less how to put her to sea!

At this point Thomas Weld met, and employed, 'Captain' Williams. He was a Weymouth man who had had 'one or two misfortunes with the Revenue' and had decided to retire from the 'free-trade line' and keep the money he had made in it.

Williams towed the vessel round to Lulworth Cove and finished her, and then the family went triumphantly for a sail to Swanage and back. This took far longer than expected as she was very slow. However, the family continued to sail in her happily enough although on one occasion they could not get out of Torbay on account of the direction of the wind and were obliged to return the sixty miles to Lulworth by land. The yacht didn't return for six weeks!

Young Joseph (he was only 8 or 9 when the yacht was launched) loved sailing and, had he not been a Roman Catholic, would almost certainly have entered the Royal Navy; unfortunately at the time the law prevented Catholics from becoming naval officers, so that avenue was closed.

However he could continue to sail his father's yacht, and there is one story from this time that seems to have set him on his future path. He was sailing to Swanage when the yacht was overtaken by one of the stone boats, one of the vessels carrying stone from Portland or Purbeck to London. These were notoriously slow, there was even a local saying, 'As slow as a Stone Boat', to describe something particularly ponderous. It is easy to imagine the hard-bitten sailors on the stone boat making rude comments on overtaking what was obviously a gentleman's yacht under full sail. This seems to have affected Joseph Weld, boys can be very sensitive to such insults, and he is said to have vowed not to be overtaken again.

In 1800, when Joseph was just 13, he and Captain Williams built another yacht on West Lulworth Beach. This yacht, called the *Castle*, was fast, incorporating ideas from the smugglers' boats, with which Captain Williams must have been well acquainted. They raced the Customs cutters along the Dorset coast – and usually won!

The *Premier* passing through a yacht race in Weymouth Bay during the early 1920s.

Eleven years later they built the *Charlotte* (named after Joseph's wife) one of the very early racing yachts. In 1815 the *Charlotte* was challenged by Mr Assheton Smith of Brownsea Island in his *Elizabeth*. This, Joseph's first match, was sailed in a very strong westerly wind and finally the *Elizabeth* got into difficulties, and the *Charlotte* towed her into Cowes. At one point Mr Smith fell overboard. This victory by the *Charlotte* won her backers nearly 2,000 guineas.

In 1812 the 'Yacht Club', was founded at Cowes with Joseph as one of its earliest members, and in 1820 it became the Royal Yacht Club. Visitors to Cowes today will see, on the walls of the Royal Yacht Squadron, long lists of the race winners going back to the earliest years of the club's history. On these early lists Joseph Weld's name appears again and again.

The Weymouth Falcons, designed as a cheap one class dingy in the 1940s, and still afloat in the harbour today.

Racing and regattas soon became part of the life of the coastal towns, these were events that catered for all classes of sailors. Races for gentlemen sailors would be intermixed with races of the local fishermen in their own boats. A regatta was held at Bournemouth as early as 1844, Lerret racing was part of the events at Weymouth in the 1850s and local fishermen were involved with racing at Christchurch in the 1860s.

Around the same time local sailing clubs were organised, the Royal Dorset Yacht Club and East Dorset Sailing Club in 1875, Christchurch Sailing Club in about 1878 and the Parkstone Yacht Club in 1895. The new sport of motor boat racing was recognised with its own organisation, the Royal Motor Yacht Club which was founded in May 1905.

Racing generally required a reasonable amount of money, but in 1926 Weymouth Sailing Club decided to remedy this by designing a class of small, reasonably priced, yachts.

> The scheme to build these boats was first mooted away back in 1926 at a committee of the Weymouth Sailing Club. Much talk and argument circled round the night's business. One fact was certain [we needed] a one design class, but the idea was weary in labour. Then a medico, wanted at a case had to leave in a hurry, but before he went the doctor stated that he was prepared to order the first of the new boats. That brief, matter-of-fact decision helped the birth.
>
> Bussell was asked to build that winter five of the new class [the Weymouth *Falcons*] their names to be, *Sparrow-Hawk, Kestrel, Kite, Peregrine* and *Buzzard*. In the spring all five were launched with a little ceremony; the new and proud owner of each boat being lowered standing up in his craft as the hulls were made ready to touch the water. The new boats proved ideal for the sailing conditions in Weymouth Bay, with mains'ls and jibs, clinker-built hulls, and varnished sides … They look a picture!

The success of these little boats can be judged by the fact that some of them can be seen in Weymouth harbour today, and they still look beautiful.

Weymouth is still a centre of sailing, and will in 2012 host the Olympic sailing events, though this time the Royal Motor Yacht Club will not be involved. In the London games of 1908 two members of the club won Olympic gold for motor boat racing, the first (and last) time this had been an Olympic event!

LITERARY VISITORS

The Dorset coast and sea has inspired many resident and visiting authors, and continues to do so. The earliest, and one of the greatest, novelists to be inspired by Dorset was Jane Austen. She had visited Lyme Regis on several occasions, in 1804 and perhaps 1805, and in her one surviving letter from the town she describes the delights of the town, including bathing and walking on the Cobb. She also felt she had been overcharged for some furniture repairs by Richard Anning, Mary's father!

She chose it as a key setting for her last novel *Persuasion*, written during 1816, and clearly she remembered the town with affection:

> After securing accommodations, and ordering a dinner at one of the inns, the next thing to be done was unquestionably to walk directly down to the sea. They were come too late in the year for any amusement or variety which Lyme, as a public place, might offer. The rooms were shut up, the lodgers almost all gone, scarcely any family but of the residents left; and, as there is nothing to admire in the buildings themselves, the remarkable situation of

the town, the principal street almost hurrying into the water, the walk to the Cobb, skirting round the pleasant little bay, which, in the season, is animated with bathing machines and company; the Cobb itself, its old wonders and new improvements...

    The party from Uppercross passing down by the now deserted and melancholy looking rooms, and still descending, soon found themselves on the sea-shore; and lingering only, as all must linger and gaze on a first return to the sea, who ever deserved to look on it at all, proceeded towards the Cobb...

The following day they returned to the Cobb.

But as they drew near the Cobb, there was such a general wish to walk along it once more...

    There was too much wind to make the high part of the new Cobb pleasant for the ladies, and they agreed to get down the steps to the lower, and all were contented to pass quietly and carefully down the steep flight, excepting Louisa; she must be jumped down them by Captain Wentworth. In all their walks, he had had to jump her from the stiles; the sensation was delightful to her. The hardness of the pavement for her feet, made him less willing upon the present occasion; he did it, however. She was safely down, and instantly, to show her enjoyment, ran up the steps to be jumped down again. He advised her against it, thought the jar too great; but no, he reasoned and talked in vain, she smiled and said, "I am determined I will:" he put out his hands; she was too precipitate by half a second, she fell on the pavement on the Lower Cobb, and was taken up lifeless! There was no wound, no blood, no visible bruise; but her eyes were closed, she breathed not, her face was like death. The horror of the moment to all who stood around!

There has been much speculation as to where exactly Jane Austen imagined Louisa Musgrove falling. 'I want to see where Louisa Musgrove fell', was apparently Tennyson's desire when he first visited Lyme Regis. However there are some difficulties, chief of which

The Gin Shop at Lyme Regis. This set of steps was built by Colonel Fanshaw in 1825

Granny's Teeth, the oldest set of steps in the Cobb, probably dating from the late seventeenth or early eighteenth century.

Louisa Musgrove's fall as drawn by Hugh Thompson in 1897. He probably never visited Lyme Regis.

is that much of the Cobb was rebuilt after its destruction in 1824. In Jane Austen's day there were probably three sets of steps from the upper level of the Cobb to the lower. The first is doubtful, it may have stood in the middle of the main pier. Here there were steps by the 'Gin Shop', just as they are today, but these were completely rebuilt in 1824. At the angle of the Cobb there is a very dramatic set of steps consisting of rocks sticking out of the Cobb wall, known as 'Granny's Teeth'; they are certainly dangerous and are frequently pointed out today as the ones where the accident happened. Finally there is a simple set of steps on the outer pier, steep and without any sort of railing.

In *Persuasion* Jane Austen describes the ladies as walking on the, 'high part of the new Cobb'. In 1804 when Jane was at Lyme Regis this can only have been the outer pier which had been rebuilt in 1792. Granny's Teeth are just beyond the end of the outer pier, so it is possible that she imagined her ladies walking there, however they are extremely steep and she described Louisa Musgrove as running up the steps. It is difficult to imagine anyone in a long dress and coat running up these steps. Therefore the most likely steps for Louisa Musgrove to have fallen from are the rather plain Outer Pier steps.

A possibly mythical visitor to the Dorset coast was the poet John Keats. Thomas Hardy believed that:

In September 1820 Keats, on his way to Rome, landed one day on the

Dorset coast, and composed the sonnet, "Bright star! would I were steadfast as thou art." The spot of his landing is judged to have been Lulworth Cove.

In fact there is some doubt that Keats wrote 'Bright Star' during a stop on the Dorset coast. Some people have considered it was written the previous year, but whatever the truth, it is a beautiful sonnet, addressed to his lover Fanny Brawne.

BRIGHT STAR

Bright star, would I were stedfast as thou art—
Not in lone splendour hung aloft the night
And watching, with eternal lids apart,
Like nature's patient, sleepless Eremite,
The moving waters at their priestlike task
Of pure ablution round earth's human shores,
Or gazing on the new soft-fallen mask
Of snow upon the mountains and the moors—
No—yet still stedfast, still unchangeable,
Pillow'd upon my fair love's ripening breast,
To feel for ever its soft fall and swell,
Awake for ever in a sweet unrest,
Still, still to hear her tender-taken breath,
And so live ever—or else swoon to death.

In 1920 Thomas Hardy used the story as the basis of a remarkable poem:

Lulworth Cove at the beginning of the nineteenth century, when Thomas Hardy imagined John Keats landing.

AT LULWORTH COVE A CENTURY BACK

Had I but lived a hundred years ago
I might have gone, as I have gone this year,
By Warmwell Cross on to a Cove I know,
And Time have placed his finger on me there:

"YOU SEE THAT MAN?"—I might have looked, and said,
"O yes: I see him. One that boat has brought
Which dropped down Channel round Saint Alban's Head.
So commonplace a youth calls not my thought."

"YOU SEE THAT MAN?"—"Why yes; I told you; yes:
Of an idling town-sort; thin; hair brown in hue;
And as the evening light scants less and less
He looks up at a star, as many do."

"YOU SEE THAT MAN?"—"Nay, leave me!" then I plead,
"I have fifteen miles to vamp across the lea,
And it grows dark, and I am weary-kneed:
I have said the third time; yes, that man I see!

"Good. That man goes to Rome—to death, despair;
And no one notes him now but you and I
A hundred years, and the world will follow him there,
And bend with reverence where his ashes lie."

Hardy describes and uses the coasts of 'Wessex' on many occasions. One example will suffice. In the short story, *The Fellow Townsmen*, he describes West Bay brilliantly:

The harbour-road soon began to justify its name. A gap appeared in the rampart of hills which shut out the sea, and on the left of the opening rose a vertical cliff, coloured a burning orange by the sunlight, the companion cliff on the right being livid in shade. Between these cliffs, like the Libyan bay which sheltered the shipwrecked Trojans, was a little haven, seemingly a beginning made by Nature herself of a perfect harbour, which appealed to the passer-by as only requiring a little human industry to finish it and make it famous, the ground on each side as fir back as the daisied slopes that bounded the interior valley being a mere layer of blown sand. But the Port-Bredy [Hardy's name for Bridport] burgesses a mile inland had, in the course of ten centuries, responded many times to that mute appeal, with the result that the tides had invariably choked up their works with sand and shingle as soon as completed. There were but few houses here: a rough pier, a few boats, some stores, an inn, a residence or two, a ketch unloading in the harbour, were the chief features of the settlement.

Occasionally the coast failed to inspire. William Barnes wrote wonderful dialect poetry describing the Dorset landscape. In 1872 he wrote a poem about Bridport Harbour. This was published in booklet form and sold for the benefit of the Bridport School of Art. The poem did not appear in early collected editions of the poet's works, and looking at the last verse one can see why.

> BRIDPORT HARBOUR
> Hill-warded haven, creek well found
> To sailors on thy stormy shore ;
> When 'midst the waters' deaf'ning roar
> They step on this thy peaceful ground,
> As blest with happy homes at hand
> Or strangers on a foreign land.
>
> As softly sinks from fear to rest
> The hunted stag, at last hound free,
> The ship that ploughs the stormy sea
> Here stills her billow-beaten breast
> And yields her welcome freight, to fill
> Her hold with works of Bridport skill.
>
> Here, fair from ev'ry shipwright's tool,
> The new ship plunges from the stocks
> And chafes her first white foam ; and rocks
> On heaving waters of thy pool,
> Now soon to waft her crest in hope
> O'er longsome tracts of sea-wide scope.
>
> The birds, where lay Prometheus bound,
> Still ate with everlasting bills
> His growing lungs, and these two hills
> So yield to eating waves their ground
> That wastes in this receding shore,
> But wastes, alas, to grow no more.
>
> How many untold years have run
> Since those two now half-hills were whole,

And man beheld the waters roll
Where they sank, grassy to the sun,
Long ere the sea had cast the sand
And far-borne pebbles on this strand.

May ev'ry ship that commerce sends
From thee, O peaceful little creek,
Come back full-rigged, without a leak,
With men to wives and friends to friends ;
May Heaven speed both to and fro
All ships that here may come and go.

The coast can inspire writers, in unexpected ways. P.D. James, the detective novelist has told how she was visiting Kimmeridge Bay Looking up at Clavel's Tower on the cliff top above, whilst other members of her party admired the view, she imagined a man in a wheelchair plummeting over the cliff. This was the initial inspiration for her story *The Black Tower*.

At the beginning of the twentieth century a boy came on holiday to Lyme Regis. He was lucky enough to find part of an ichthyosaur jaw. Though he knew what it really was he labelled it 'Dragons Jaw'. He had a right to for the boy was J.R.R. Tolkien, who was to create the finest dragon in modern English literature.

Whatever changes on the Dorset coast, one thing is certain, it will continue to delight and inspire people long into the future.

Sources and Further Reading

As will be appreciated a great many other authors have been consulted and quoted throughout this book. The principal ones are:

Bell, A. 1916 *From Harbour To Harbour.*
Brown, H. R. 1855 *The Beauties of Lyme Regis, Charmouth, the Land-Slip and their vicinities.*
Clunn, H. 1929 *Famous South Coast Pleasure Resorts – Past and Present.*
Defoe, D. 1724-7 *A tour through the whole island of Great Britain.*
Drayton, M. 1612 *Polyolbion.*
Ellis, G. A. 1839 *The History and Antiquities of the Borough and town of Weymouth and Melcombe Regis.*
Farr, G. 1971 *Wreck and Rescue on the Dorset Coast.*
Fiennes, C. 1949 *Through England on a Side Saddle in the time of William and Mary.*
Gerard, T. 1732 *A Survey of Dorsetshire.*
Granville, A. B. 1841 *The Spas of England, Principal Sea-Bathing Places.*
Hill, E. G. 1912 *Fanny Burney at the court of Queen Charlotte.*
Hutchins, J. 1774 *History and Antiquities of the County of Dorset.*
Page, W. 1908 *Victoria History Of The County Of Dorset. Vol.2.*
Payne-Gallwey, Ralph. 1893 *The Diary of Colonel Peter Hawker.*
Roberts, G. 1834 *The history and antiquities of the borough of Lyme Regis and Charmouth.*
Smith, C. 1796 *Narrative of the loss of the* Catharine, Venus, *and* Piedmont *transports*
Sydenham, J. 1839 *The History of the Town and County of Poole.*

PICTURES

The pictures are all from my own collection, apart from the aerial photographs for which I must thank Dorset County Council.